W9-BVC-599

THE
STATUE OF
LIBERTY

BUILDING
HISTORY
SERIES

THE
STATUE OF
LIBERTY

by Russell Roberts

Lucent Books, an imprint of The Gale Group

On cover: (left) The statue during
New York Construction, 1886;
(top right) The Statue of Liberty;
(bottom right) A plaster cast for
the Statue of Liberty.

To Pat—
Another great girl

Library of Congress Cataloging-in-Publication Data

Roberts, Russell, 1953–
  The Statue of Liberty / by Russell Roberts.
    p.   cm. — (Building history series)
Includes bibliographical references and index.
  ISBN 1-56006-841-8 (hardback : alk. paper)
  1. Statue of Liberty (New York, N.Y.)—History—Juvenile
literature. 2. Statue of Liberty National Monument (N.Y. and
N.J.)—Juvenile literature. 3. New York (N.Y.)—Buildings,
structures, etc.—Juvenile literature. [1. Statue of Liberty (New
York, N.Y.) 2. National monuments. 3. New York (N.Y.)—
Buildings, structures, etc.] I. Title. II. Series.
  F128.64.L6 R63   2002
  974.7'1—dc21

2001001770

Printed in the U.S.A.

CONTENTS

FOREWORD

Throughout history, as civilizations have evolved and prospered, each has produced unique buildings and architectural styles. Combining the need for both utility and artistic expression, a society's buildings, particularly its large-scale public structures, often reflect the individual character traits that distinguish it from other societies. In a very real sense, then, buildings express a society's values and unique characteristics in tangible form. As scholar Anita Abramovitz comments in her book *People and Spaces*, "Our ways of living and thinking—our habits, needs, fear of enemies, aspirations, materialistic concerns, and religious beliefs—have influenced the kinds of spaces that we build and that later surround and include us."

That specific types and styles of structures constitute an outward expression of the spirit of an individual people or era can be seen in the diverse ways that various societies have built palaces, fortresses, tombs, churches, government buildings, sports arenas, public works, and other such monuments. The ancient Greeks, for instance, were a supremely rational people who originated Western philosophy and science, including the atomic theory and the realization that the earth is a sphere. Their public buildings, epitomized by Athens's magnificent Parthenon temple, were equally rational, emphasizing order, harmony, reason, and above all, restraint.

By contrast, the Romans, who conquered and absorbed the Greek lands, were a highly practical people preoccupied with acquiring and wielding power over others. The Romans greatly admired and readily copied elements of Greek architecture, but modified and adapted them to their own needs. "Roman genius was called into action by the enormous practical needs of a world empire," wrote historian Edith Hamilton. "Rome met them magnificently. Buildings tremendous, indomitable, amphitheaters where eighty thousand could watch a spectacle, baths where three thousand could bathe at the same time."

In medieval Europe, God heavily influenced and motivated the people, and religion permeated all aspects of society, molding people's worldviews and guiding their everyday actions. That spiritual mindset is reflected in the most important medieval structure—the Gothic cathedral—which, in a sense, was a model of heavenly cities. As scholar Anne Fremantle so elegantly phrases it, the cathedrals were "harmonious elevations of stone and glass reaching up to heaven to seek and receive the light [of God]."

Our more secular modern age, in contrast, is driven by the realities of a global economy, advanced technology, and mass communications. Responding to the needs of international trade and the growth of cities housing millions of people, today's builders construct engineering marvels, among them towering skyscrapers of steel and glass, mammoth marine canals, and huge and elaborate rapid transit systems, all of which would have left their ancestors, even the Romans, awestruck.

In examining some of humanity's greatest edifices, Lucent Books' Building History series recognizes this close relationship between a society's historical character and its buildings. Each volume in the series begins with a historical sketch of the people who erected the edifice, exploring their major achievements as well as the beliefs, customs, and societal needs that dictated the variety, functions, and styles of their buildings. A detailed explanation of how the selected structure was conceived, designed, and built, to the extent that this information is known, makes up the majority of the volume.

Each volume in the Lucent Building History series also includes several special features that are useful tools for additional research. A chronology of important dates gives students an overview, at a glance, of the evolution and use of the structure described. Sidebars create a broader context by adding further details on some of the architects, engineers, and construction tools, materials, and methods that made each structure a reality, as well as the social, political, and/or religious leaders and movements that inspired its creation. Useful maps help the reader locate the nations, cities, streets, and individual structures mentioned in the text; and numerous diagrams and pictures illustrate tools and devices that bring to life various stages of construction. Finally, each volume contains two bibliographies, one for student research, the other listing works the author consulted in compiling the book.

Taken as a whole, these volumes, covering diverse ancient and modern structures, constitute not only a valuable research tool, but also a tribute to the human spirit, a fascinating exploration of the dreams, skills, ingenuity, and dogged determination of the great peoples who shaped history.

Important Dates in the Building of the Statue of Liberty

1834
Frédéric-Auguste Bartholdi is born in Colmar, France.

1865
The idea of France giving America a gift celebrating liberty is discussed at a dinner party given by Édouard-René Lefebvre de Laboulaye.

1855
Bartholdi designs a statue of General Rapp for the city of Colmar.

1870
The Franco-Prussian War begins.

1871
Bartholdi visits the U.S. to gain support for the statue.

1876
Bartholdi completes the right arm and the torch and sends it to the Philadelphia Centennial Exposition.

1879
Alexandre-Gustave Eiffel replaces Viollet-le-Duc following his death. He begins designing the internal supports for the statue.

| 1834 | 1855 | 1865 | 1870 | 1871 | 1875 | 1876 | 1878 | 1879 | 1880 | 1881 |

The Statue of Liberty towers over New York Harbor.

1875
The Franco-American Union is formed in France to raise money to build the statue. Bartholdi begins work on the statue.

1878
The statue's head is completed for display in Paris.

1880
The Franco-American Union completes raising money.

1881
Outdoor assembly of the statue begins in Paris. Richard Morris Hunt is named architect of the pedestal.

1980
An illegal climb of the statue prompts officials to inspect it.
The need for a massive maintenance effort is revealed.

1924
Statue is designated a national monument.

1886
Pedestal is completed. The statue is dedicated
on Bedloe's Island.

1984
The statue is
closed to the public
for renovations.

1884
Assembly of the statue
is complete.

1904
Bartholdi dies.

1883	1884	1885	1886	1901	1904	1916	1924	1956	1980	1982	1984	1986

1956
Bedloe's Island is renamed
Liberty Island.

1902
The War Department
becomes responsible for
the care of the statue.

1982
The Statue of
Liberty–Ellis
Island Centen-
nial Commis-
sion is formed to
spearhead the
fund-raising for
the statue's
maintenance.

1986
The statue is reopened.

1885
The statue is disassembled
and shipped to America.
Pulitzer begins raising
money for the pedestal.

1883
Laboulaye dies on May 25.

1916
Tiny squares of amber glass
are added to the flame in an
effort to increase its visibility.

INTRODUCTION

It sits in New York Harbor, a giant copper colossus holding aloft a torch that symbolizes the light of liberty that illuminates the United States of America.

The Statue of Liberty, sculpted by Frédéric-Auguste Bartholdi (pictured), was a gift from France to the United States representing the values of freedom and independence.

It is the Statue of Liberty—a gift from France to America celebrating the friendship between the two countries. The statue was born out of a casual dinner party conversation—an attempt to deepen and strengthen the bonds between France and the United States. It has become the unofficial symbol of America, a robed woman representing the ideals of freedom and independence upon which this country was founded.

Yet the Statue of Liberty has also become something more. In its simple elegance, it has become a welcoming beacon to millions of immigrants. It represents a land of opportunity, where people can be themselves and live and work in peace.

The statue's journey to America was a strange one. Beset by money woes almost constantly prior to construction, the Statue of Liberty was initially greeted in this country by a collective yawn. Money woes haunted the statue in America too, and the magnificent pedestal upon which it stands was only built thanks to a newspaper publisher's determination and the small monetary gifts of thousands of ordinary people.

The statue has stood in New York Harbor for over a century, acting as a beacon of freedom for people not only in the United States but throughout the world. It has not been an easy existence: The statue's light has never worked as intended—despite constant repairs—and it needed a massive facelift in the 1980s. And yet still it survives. Like the United States itself, the Statue of Liberty has only become stronger despite the adversity it has suffered.

A Dinner Party Conversation

Seeking a way to honor the relationship between France and America, the French professor Édouard-René Lefebvre de Laboulaye had the idea of creating a monument to celebrate America's basic principles of individual freedom and liberty. A sculptor, Frédéric-Auguste Bartholdi, was chosen to create the statue. But much time passed as the two waited for the right moment in the politically unstable climate of France to raise money for the statue. During this time, however, Bartholdi took the opportunity to design what would become one of America's most recognized monuments.

French-American Relations Throughout History

Throughout its history, the United States has always had a strong relationship with the nation of France. It was the intervention of France, after all, that enabled America to secure its independence from Great Britain. The timely intervention of French troops and the French navy during the Revolutionary War helped America fight England on more equal terms and eventually convinced the British to abandon the war. In fact, the French fleet prevented the English from retreating at Yorktown and helped America win that decisive victory.

By the mid-1860s, however, the French nation that had once helped America was gone. In its place was a dictatorship under the rule of Napoléon III. He had overthrown the Second Republic in 1852, and his government was the ninth in France since the French Revolution of the 1780s had toppled the monarchy of Louis XVI.

Napoléon III was not a friend to the United States. In fact, during the American Civil War he was an open Confederate sympathizer. His regime was repressive to the people, and it was openly hostile to individual rights. For example, he had special commissioners survey all imported printed material to determine if it was a threat to his autocratic rule.

For those in France who wanted a republican (democracy) form of government, these were dark days. Several prominent supporters of democracy were interested in bringing liberty back to France, however, including Laboulaye. A law professor at the Collège de France and a leading republican, Laboulaye wanted to establish a democratic form of government similar to that of the United States, which he greatly admired. He had been one of the leading supporters of the Union during the American Civil War, and the American ambassador to France, John Bigelow, reported that Laboulaye's pro-Union writings were one of the major reasons France did not officially support the Confederacy during the war.

Napoléon III ruled France as a dictator in the 1860s.

In fact, French republicans like Laboulaye had led a secret subscription drive to strike a gold medal in Abraham Lincoln's honor after he was assassinated in 1865. Even after Napoléon III seized the money and the list of subscribers to the medal, Laboulaye had the medal made anyway and sent it to America. Republicans who sent the medal to Lincoln's widow also sent along a note saying, "In this little box is the heart of France."[1] Many French republicans felt that the recently concluded Civil War had once again shown how far America would go for the cause of liberty. Americans had spilled copious amounts of their own blood to end slavery, which Lincoln had established as one of the North's goals during the Civil War.

A MEMORABLE DINNER PARTY

In the summer of 1865 Laboulaye hosted a dinner party at which one of the topics for discussion was an idea for a way to commemorate America. One guest asserted that no nation ever

ÉDOUARD-RENÉ LEFEBVRE DE LABOULAYE

Born in 1811, Édouard-René Lefebvre de Laboulaye rose to become the greatest orator and the staunchest defender of the republican tradition in France during the turbulent period after the Franco-Prussian War. Laboulaye gave one of the greatest speeches in French history while a member of the General Assembly in 1875, entering the debate over which type of government France should have with an eloquent plea for a republic. He ended his speech with a memorable request for the delegates to have pity on France and to adopt a republican form of government. His speech made a tremendous impact; France adopted a republican form of government a few days later.

appreciated help from another, but Laboulaye denied this. He felt that the United States would always appreciate France's help in winning its independence.

"The American nation," Laboulaye said, "has more sympathy for France than for any other European nation." Then he brought up a unique idea: France should create something honoring America's commitment to freedom and liberty and present it to the United States in time for that nation's one hundredth birthday celebration in 1876. Said Laboulaye to his dinner guests, "If a monument should rise in the United States, as a memorial to their independence, I should think it only natural if it were built by united effort—a common work of both our nations."[2]

But nothing happened concerning the gift that night, nor would anything happen in the following years. In the meantime, American-French relations deteriorated, due in part to the Franco-Prussian War.

NAPOLÉON III AND THE FRANCO-PRUSSIAN WAR

Napoléon III proved to have only his famous predecessor's name, not his military cunning. In 1870 he was lured into a war with Prussia over the attempt to put Leopold, prince of Hohenzollern-Sigmaringen (a German state), on the Spanish throne. The chancellor of Prussia, Otto von Bismarck, wanted to unite all of the German states into a single country, and he felt that a war would accomplish this. It was Bismarck who was behind Leopold.

France already had German states on its eastern border. If the move to put Leopold on the Spanish throne succeeded, France would have a German state on her southern border as well. This was intolerable to Napoléon III, and after various diplomatic maneuvers failed, France attacked Prussia on July 15, 1870.

Although Napoléon III took personal command of the French army, he lacked military skill and ability. When he proved unable to transport his army across the Rhine River, he set himself and France up for a disastrous defeat, which occurred on September 1, 1870, at the Battle of Sedan in northern France.

The loss sealed France's fate; the war was lost. France was forced to sign the humiliating Treaty of Frankfurt with Prussia in May 1871. As a result, France lost the territories of Alsace and part of Lorraine and had to pay Prussia 5 billion francs in compensation.

When some groups of Frenchmen heard about the peace treaty they were furious over its terms and formed a new government (Napoléon III had been forced into exile). This did not

French soldiers stand behind a barricade in a street in Paris during the Franco-Prussian War.

sit well with those who wanted to form a royalist government (when a monarch such as a king or queen is in charge), and the two sides fought. In one week thirty thousand Frenchmen were shot by the army under the direction of the republicans.

The United States treated the Franco-Prussian War and its aftermath with indifference. New York City sent some provisions to Paris when it was under attack by the Prussians, but otherwise the entire war was a virtual nonevent in America. This made Laboulaye and his republican allies even more inclined to design a gift for America.

Laboulaye still felt that an American-style government was the best for France; when Napoléon III abdicated, Laboulaye saw his chance to bring democracy to France. He also wanted to rekindle the spark of warm feelings that the two nations had once had for each other, and so he revived the idea of a gift from France to America. In reality, the gift would have several purposes: It would not only be France's way of honoring the U.S. commitment to personal freedom, but it would also be a way of saying "happy birthday" to America (and hopefully warm up American-French relations). First, however, a person had to be chosen to create the gift: The choice was a sculptor named Frédéric-Auguste Bartholdi.

BARTHOLDI

Born in Colmar, France, in the province of Alsace on April 2, 1834, Bartholdi was raised in a prosperous middle-class family.

NAPOLÉON III

Born in 1808, Charles-Louis-Napoléon Bonaparte was the third son of King Louis and Queen Hortense of Holland and a nephew of Napoléon Bonaparte. A fervent believer in the Bonaparte family's right to rule France, he won the French presidency in 1848 following the ouster of King Louis Philippe. He led a government takeover in 1851, assuming dictatorial powers. However, after 1860 he began liberalizing his regime. He led an ill-prepared France in a war against Prussia in 1870, France was swiftly defeated, and Napoléon was removed from power. He died in exile in 1873.

THE FRANCO-PRUSSIAN WAR

Fought by Emperor Napoléon III in a futile attempt to regain French influence in Europe and particularly in Germany, the war was fought between 1870 and 1871. The event that triggered the war was the candidacy of Leopold, prince of Hohenzollern-Sigmaringen, for the vacant throne of Spain. He was Prussia's candidate, and Napoléon was afraid of a Spanish-Prussian alliance. Even though Leopold withdrew his candidacy, France was determined to humiliate Prussia, and it demanded a personal letter of apology from the Prussian king, William I. He refused, and France declared war on July 19, 1870. The decisive Battle of Sedan occurred in early September, followed by the capitulation of Paris in January. By then Napoléon III had been ousted, and a new French government was formed.

Prussian troops gained the advantage over the French during the Battle of Sedan.

When he was a young man he showed a talent for art and drawing, and he enrolled as a student of the painter Ary Scheffer. When Scheffer advised him to study sculpture, Bartholdi began working with the sculptor Jean-François Soitux. He also studied architecture under Eugène-Emmanuel Viollet-le-Duc, a world-renowned engineer.

During this time Bartholdi also fought in the Franco-Prussian War, with unforeseen consequences for both America and France.

Sculptor Frédéric-Auguste Bartholdi employed a broad, simple style in his work.

He tried to defend his hometown of Colmar, but France wound up surrendering it to the Prussians. Under the terms of the peace treaty, France lost Bartholdi's homeland of Alsace to Prussia. Bartholdi was extremely bitter over the loss and considered Alsace to be occupied territory for the rest of his life. He never visited Alsace again, except to pay his mother an occasional call. This showed him firsthand how damaging a despot's reign could be, and the experience made him eager to produce a monument to freedom and liberty.

In addition to his political motivations, Bartholdi had one driving, motivating passion: He was enamored with creating large-size works. "I have a horror of all frippery of detail in sculpture," he once said. "The forms and effects of that art should be broad, massive and simple."[3]

He put his philosophy into practice early. In fact, prior to fighting in the Franco-Prussian War (when he was just nineteen years old), the city of Colmar commissioned him to create a twelve-foot-high statue of General Jean de Rapp, a Colmar native who became an aide to Napoléon. The work was highly praised and started Bartholdi on a career as a successful sculptor.

Being a successful artist, single, young, and dashing, with piercing eyes, Bartholdi quickly became a much sought-after guest at parties. Thus, he was present at Laboulaye's 1865 dinner party when the idea emerged of a gift from France to the United States. Later, when it was determined that the gift would be a statue, Bartholdi was selected as the sculptor. Because of his love of the colossal, he decided to create a giant statue in America's honor.

A Sign of the Times

Large statues celebrating values were in vogue at this time, and Bartholdi became one of colossal statuary's biggest proponents.

"The abundance of commemorative statues is a characteristic sign of this era,"[4] wrote a journalist.

During the late nineteenth century, people were rediscovering the power and beauty of such ancient wonders as the Egyptian pyramids and the legendary statue of the Colossus of Rhodes (a giant figure of the Greek god Helios straddling the entrance to the harbor of the island of Rhodes, under whose legs ships supposedly sailed to enter the harbor). The appeal of these classical structures merged with Bartholdi's desire to create a giant sculpture.

The sculptor had numerous other models from which to draw inspiration. In 1766 a great equestrian statue of Peter the Great was produced in St. Petersburg, Russia, and in 1850 a huge figure representing the Germanic state of Bavaria was made in Munich, Germany. Bartholdi also drew inspiration from the many classic buildings in the United States, including Thomas Jefferson's home at Monticello, George Washington's home at Mount Vernon, and many of the buildings in Washington, D.C.

A PRECURSOR TO THE STATUE OF LIBERTY?

The idea to portray a giant robed woman had not suddenly sprung from Bartholdi's head. He had tried once before to create such a statue. In 1867 he had proposed the creation of a 132-foot-tall lighthouse and pedestal at the entrance to the Suez Canal, which was then being built. The proposal called for the lighthouse to be in the form of a giant robed woman holding a torch. It was called *Egypt Carrying the Light to Asia*. The proposal, however, died for a lack of funds on Egypt's part, and Bartholdi sadly packed away his plans and dreams.

When the chance came to create a monument to American liberty as well as a lighthouse (it was thought that making the statue functional would help America accept it), some critics felt he simply dusted off his old plans for the Suez lighthouse, made some necessary changes, and renamed the statue *Liberty Enlightening the World*.

However, Bartholdi was very sensitive about the close resemblance between the Egyptian statue and the monument to American liberty. He vigorously denied that the two were similar at all, saying that there was only one common feature: "Both held a light aloft. Now . . . how is a sculptor to make a statue, which is to serve the purpose of a lighthouse, without holding that light in the air? Would they have me make the figure . . . hiding the light under its petticoat?"[5]

BARTHOLDI COMES TO AMERICA

Before Bartholdi designed his great statue, he decided to visit America "to succeed in realizing my plan for the monument in honor of Independence."[6] In a letter to Laboulaye asking for support, Bartholdi wrote,

> I will try especially to glorify the Republic and Liberty over there, hoping that I will one day find them back here, if possible. I hope, on my return, to find my poor France a little relieved of those angry, many-colored boils that formed and burst because of the Empire.[7]

Bartholdi did receive the illustrious professor's support, in the form of letters of introduction to people in the United States. Laboulaye told him,

> Go to see that country. Propose to our friends over there to make with us a monument, a common work, in re- membrance of the ancient friendship of France and the United States. If . . . you find a plan that will excite pub- lic enthusiasm, we are convinced that it will be success- ful on both continents, and we will do a work that will have far-reaching moral effect.[8]

On June 8, 1871, Bartholdi sailed for America aboard the steamship *Pereire*. When he initially sailed into New York Har- bor on June 21, he was struck by a vision: He instantly saw that the harbor was the ideal location for his statue. As he stated, "The image presented to the sight of a passenger arriving is splendid."[9]

Bartholdi immediately knew the spiritual effect his statue would have on the many immigrants and others who arrived in America via the harbor. "If I myself felt that spirit here," Bartholdi wrote, "then it is certainly here that my statue must rise; here where people get their first view of the New World, and where Liberty casts her rays on both worlds."[10]

The sculptor had even found the ideal spot in the harbor for his statue: a neglected little island named Bedloe's Island. He wrote at the time,

An illustration shows a busy New York Harbor in 1870, before the arrival of the Statue of Liberty.

I've found an admirable spot. It is Bedloe's Island, in the middle of the bay. I've made a little drawing of the work as it would look when emplaced there. The island belongs to the government; it's on national territory, belonging to all the States, just opposite the Narrows, which are, so to speak, the gateway to America.[11]

He went on to say,

At the view of the Harbor of New York, the definite plan was first clear to my eyes . . . in the pearly radiance of a beautiful morning is revealed the magnificent spectacle of those immense cities, of those rivers extending as far as the eye can reach. . . . In this very place shall be raised the Statue of Liberty, grand as the idea which it embodies, radiant upon the two worlds.[12]

Bartholdi wrote a letter to Laboulaye and enclosed a sketch showing a gigantic robed woman holding a torch with the light of liberty emanating from her head in separate, individual rays. Laboulaye, who had envisioned something more tangible about American-French relations, would eventually come around to the sculptor's point of view about his statue.

MEETING PEOPLE

During his visit to America, Bartholdi spent a few weeks in New York City. However, he soon embarked on a busy travel schedule. He wanted to travel around the United States as much as possible. He had picked the ideal time in which to see America. Everywhere he looked the country was alive and burning with energy. The nation had emerged from the horrors of the Civil War ready to return to work. Men were working in factories, forests, mines, and stores; out west, ranchers were battling the forces of nature while great cattle drives moved across their lands. Bartholdi saw it all: the older, more established cities like New York and Philadelphia and the newer towns like Chicago and Denver. Bartholdi also saw the natural beauty of the country, such as Niagara Falls and the giant sequoia trees of California.

While he was marveling at the country, he did not neglect his primary purpose, which was meeting people and drumming up support for the statue. "I seek in each town," he wrote to Laboulaye, "individuals willing to take part in our enterprise. Up to now I have found some everywhere."[13] He met politicians such as President Ulysses S. Grant and the abolitionist senator Charles Sumner from Massachusetts. He also met America's unofficial poet laureate, Henry Wadsworth Longfellow. In every city and town he visited, Bartholdi sought out the most influential people and tried to interest them in supporting his statue.

THE WRONG TIME

By the time he returned to France in early 1872, Bartholdi realized that some practical gesture was needed to keep interest alive in America. He had talked incessantly about his statue and had done a good job of sparking interest in it. Now he had to prove that he was not just a talkative Frenchman with a pie-in-the-sky idea of a giant statue, but that he could actually deliver it.

But the timing was all wrong. In France, Laboulaye's republican supporters tenuously held the reins of power. The French people were being heavily taxed to pay for the money they owed the Prussian government as a result of the peace treaty that ended the Franco-Prussian War. It was hardly the time to launch any type of fund-raising effort to pay for the new statue or a public campaign to provide a gift to the United States. One misstep could sink the republican government.

So Bartholdi bided his time. He worked on other projects, such as a bronze statue of Lafayette commissioned by French president Louis-Adolphe Thiers for the people of New York City to thank them for their support during the Franco-Prussian War. Other projects included a cast-iron fountain for Philadelphia and a series of sculptures of great Americans for a Boston church.

In his spare time, however, he continued to work on what he now called "my American,"[14] making drawings and small models so he would know exactly what the statue would look like when it came time to begin the actual work. He already knew the basic design of the project. As he stated at the time,

> [The statue should be] "read easily" at the distance at which it will be seen, it is essential that its movement be simple and that it display in silhouette almost unbroken lines . . . and in the actual model, major planes in which individual planes are dissolved and lost.[15]

DETAILS OF THE STATUE

Although he had a general sense of the style he wanted for the statue, the details were much harder for Bartholdi to determine. He was perplexed over how to depict the concept of liberty. He did not know whether he should show it as a woman, as was done in ancient Roman times. He also had his Egyptian lighthouse design to take into account.

Likewise, he had to consider the element of freemasonry. Bartholdi was a freemason himself, having joined the lodge of Alsace-Lorraine (the two French provinces lost in the Franco-Prussian War). In France, the freemasons were a powerful political force. Often taking liberal positions that even Laboulaye would not support, the freemasons were one of the leading bastions of the republican movement in France. At the time, the magazine of the French freemasons depicted the concept of truth as a woman with a five-pointed star on her head standing on a pedestal as the sun shines behind her.

Bartholdi was inspired by other models of liberty as well. Over the Bastille, a French prison, was the *Genius of Liberty*, which showed a male figure carrying a flaming torch in one hand and a broken chain in the other. A famous painting of the time by Eugène Delacroix was *Liberty Leading the People*, which depicted a young woman with a flag in her right hand and a musket in her left hand leading a pack of revolutionaries. And there was also

Columbia, the unofficial symbol of the United States, who was always a woman and who always wore a robe.

After carefully considering his options, Bartholdi chose a woman to represent liberty. However, he also had to decide what the statue should be holding. He finally selected a torch for the right hand to represent the sacred enlightening force of liberty. For the left hand, he decided on a tablet inscribed with the date of the Declaration of Independence in Roman numerals: July IV MDCCLXXVI (July 4, 1776). Only to Americans would such a date be significant.

The Statue of Liberty's headdress was another consideration. Bartholdi was uncertain whether to have the statue hold or wear a Phrygian cap. (In ancient times Phrygian caps were given to slaves when they gained their freedom.) A cap had come to be associated with the radical and ruthless elements of the French Rev-

The bold spirit of Eugène Delacroix's painting, Liberty Leading the People, *inspired Bartholdi's work.*

olution, and Bartholdi did not want to stir up memories of that sad conflict. Eventually the sculptor settled on a crown from which seven rays emitted. The rays could either signify the seven continents or the seven seas. A sunburst, which the crown resembled, was also the emblem of the Bartholdi family.

There was another advantage to choosing the crown. Bartholdi figured he could put windows in it, through which light could shine on the water below. This would fulfill the lighthouse function.

Bartholdi also debated about how to show an intangible quality such as independence. He considered using a cat (a traditional symbol for independence) at the feet of the statue as well as the figure of liberty stepping on a broken pitcher, which was a symbol of breaking free from slavery. Broken chains were also a commonly recognized symbol of victory over slavery. Bartholdi liked the symbolism, but he did not want it to be too prominent, such as having the figure holding the chains in her hand. Instead, he decided to depict the statue stepping on the chains. Again, however, he did not want to make the depiction too obvious. He experimented with several different ways of depicting the shattered chains, at one point wrapping them around the base of the statue. Eventually, though, Bartholdi decided that even that was too conspicuous, and so he chose to hide them under the figure's robes, thus making them barely visible.

IMPRESSIVE DIMENSIONS

Bartholdi made the decision to build his "American" to a rather majestic height of 151 feet (from the base to the torch). He wanted his monument to liberty to be imposing. A figure that tall would require impressive dimensions, but Bartholdi was prepared. He determined that the waist would have to be thirty-five feet thick; the face, ten feet wide; and the nose, four feet long.

Bartholdi also pondered long and hard about which way the statue would face. He finally placed it in a south-southeasterly direction. Seen from this vantage point (the right side by incoming ships), the statue at first seems to be striding forward. But then, as the view changes to the front, the statue does not appear to be moving at all and seems serenely at rest.

COPPER IS THE CHOICE

After determining the size, Bartholdi turned his attention to the type of material he would use to make the statue. Bronze or stone was not possible for a work of such size because it was too heavy. Eventually he chose copper because it was light, inexpensive, and easy to work with. The sculptor then turned to the ancient technique of copper repoussé (which means "pushed back").

Copper repoussé statues are essentially hollow shells. In the copper repoussé method, thin sheets of copper are hammered against hard plaster molds in the shape of the statue. The molds are made by fashioning wet plaster around clay shapes and allowing the plaster to dry. Once the copper is formed into the desired shape, it needs an internal skeleton, called the supporting armature, on which to be hung.

Bartholdi had an existing model to study for the copper repoussé method. A statue of Saint Charles Borromeo, a sixteenth-century archbishop from Milan, Italy, situated on the shore of Lake Maggiore in northern Italy, had been produced during the seventeenth century by the same method. It was seventy-six feet high and was almost hollow, yet it had lasted two centuries (at that time), surviving every force of nature. Bartholdi's statue would be nearly twice as high.

Surviving the elements was important to Bartholdi. In the saltwater-laden air of New York Harbor, fully exposed to the elements, the statue would have to endure nature's fury. A statue made via the repoussé method can move, sway, and bend without fear of damage because it is so lightweight.

Once the copper repoussé method had been selected, the sculptor had to determine the thickness of the copper to use. Tests and calculations were made, and it was decided that the copper would have to be $3/32$ of an inch thick—about the width of two pennies placed side to side.

SUPPORTING THE STATUE

Before he could actually start building the statue, Bartholdi needed a structural frame upon which to hang the sheets of copper. The frame needed to be lightweight enough to bend and withstand wind, rain, and whatever else nature might unleash upon the statue, but it also needed to be strong enough to hold the weight of the metal.

For this important job he selected the renowned French architect (and his old teacher) Eugène-Emmanuel Viollet-le-Duc. Viollet-le-Duc's plan for supporting the statue was to design an inner section composed of compartments filled with sand. Each compartment was designed so that it could stand alone—that is, each compartment could be emptied of the sand if repairs were needed to the "skin," or copper sheeting, for that particular compartment. It was his plan to fill the statue with sand up to its waist, then build a light frame to support the upper half of the statue.

THE MYSTERY OF THE FACE

Once all of these details were finalized, Bartholdi had to select a model for his statue. Because he never told anyone who his model was, there has been a great deal of speculation about it.

One story is that he selected his mother, Charlotte. This is given credence by an anecdote told by a French senator. It seems that he and Bartholdi were going to the opera together. When the senator entered the opera house, he noticed an aged woman and exclaimed, "Why, that's your model for the Statue of Liberty!" Bartholdi answered, "Yes, it's my mother."[16]

Another person Bartholdi may have chosen as a model was a young woman named Jeanne-Emilie Baheux, whom Bartholdi eventually married. But he knew her only slightly during the time

Architect Eugène-Emmanuel Viollet-le-Duc, designed the structural framework for the Statue of Liberty.

he was finishing the design for the statue, and only in 1876 did he renew his friendship with her. (The couple was married in late December 1876.) However, it is unlikely that she was the model since the two were separated by an ocean during the exact time when the sculptor was designing the statue, and she would have had to pose for him. (She was in the United States, and he was in France.) Some sources say that Baheux was in Paris working as a dressmaker's assistant at this time and that Bartholdi had her pose for the body of the statue, but it is unknown if this is accurate.

A few other speculations exist about the statue's face. One is that the face is that of Mrs. Isaac Singer, the widow of the inventor of the sewing machine. However, she resettled in Paris in 1878, too late for her face to be used as the model. Bartholdi also allowed a rumor to circulate that the statue somewhat resembled a

Bartholdi is photographed working diligently in his Paris studio.

young girl whom he had seen shot down in a street riot in 1851. No one knows whether this is true. It is always possible that the Statue of Liberty has the face of a model that Bartholdi hired. This is what one author contends, and he identifies the girl as being named Celine.

No one knows which, if any, of these stories is true. Bartholdi took this information to his grave. It is likely that we will never know whose face actually adorns the Statue of Liberty.

Once the sculptor had decided on all of these details, he was ready to build his "American." What Bartholdi did not know was that he would be plagued by money troubles for several years, and that building the statue would often take a back seat to the task of fund-raising. He did not know that America's indifference and own money troubles would lead to the statue almost not having a pedestal upon which to stand.

A Slow Start

The next step in Bartholdi's and Laboulaye's quest to build a gift for America was finding enough money for the project. Laboulaye formed a group, the Franco-American Union, which held various fund-raising efforts for the statue. Figuring that France was footing the bill for the statue, he persuaded America to pay for the pedestal. But still French fund-raising efforts were not enough, and Bartholdi had to constantly involve himself in raising money as the costs of building his "American" escalated. Meanwhile, the initial burst of enthusiasm for the statue had faded in America, and Bartholdi found that he had to play one city against another to get New Yorkers excited anew about the project. The city's attitude mirrored that of the rest of the country, which seemed alternately excited, then perplexed, about the statue.

For Want of a Flag

Politically, the time was finally right to begin the project. By the spring of 1875 the republicans were firmly in control of the French government. They had won control over a seemingly trivial matter. Early in the 1870s those who wanted to restore the monarchy were on the verge of reestablishing a king as head of the government. Their choice for king was the count of Chambord. The count was a descendant of the Bourbon dynasty, which had ruled France until the French Revolution toppled it in 1789. The count was so positive that he would become king that he began signing his correspondence "Henri V of France."

However, the return of the monarchy fell apart over the colors of the flag. Ever since the French Revolution the country's flag had consisted of three broad stripes of red, white, and blue, known as the tricolor. The French people were very happy with and proud of this flag, feeling that it signified their triumph over an unjust king. But the count of Chambord refused to become king under this flag. To him, the flag was a symbol of violence and revolution. He wanted the old Bourbon flag restored, which was white with three flowers on it.

The monarchists were horrified by his request. They explained that the people were quite fond of their existing flag and to go back to the old one was political suicide. But the count did not care. So, over an issue so minor as the color of the flag, the monarchists' plans collapsed.

Thus, by early 1875 Laboulaye and his liberals had won control of the French parliament. Laboulaye gave a powerful speech to the parliament in which he pleaded for a republican form of government. His proposal passed, and a new constitution was written defining France as a republic forever.

THE FRANCO-AMERICAN UNION

With the political situation under control and the design of the statue decided upon, Laboulaye and Bartholdi felt that the time was right to proceed with the project. First, however, they needed to raise money. In April 1875 Laboulaye established the Franco-American Union as a means of raising money for the statue. Laboulaye was the president of the group, and other important people were members, including Elihu Washburne, the American ambassador to France; Philippe Bartholdi, the French ambassador to the United States and a distant cousin of the sculptor; John W. Forney, commissioner general of the United States in Europe for the Philadelphia Centennial Exposition; and members of some of France's finest families, such as the Lafayettes.

AMERICA IN THE 1870S

The America that Bartholdi visited in 1871 was bursting with energy and enthusiasm. The traumatic Civil War had ended, and the country was rapidly leaving it behind. Everywhere there was activity—factories were being built in the old eastern cities like Baltimore and Boston, and new cities like Houston and Denver were being built out west. Except for the recession of 1873 and its effects, the American economic engine was roaring. Robber barons (capitalists who became wealthy through exploitation) such as financiers Jay Gould and James Fisk held sway in many industries, and inventors like Thomas Edison and Alexander Graham Bell were working in their laboratories, ready to unleash the electric light, the telephone, and other inventions that would change the world.

After opening a bank account and establishing an office, the union printed its first public appeal for money in two Paris newspapers on September 28, 1875. The appeal stated that an important event in human history was approaching with America's one hundredth anniversary. It also said that a French artist had devised a gigantic statue for New York Harbor to mark the occasion. The appeal went on to state, "On the threshold of that vast continent, full of new life, where ships arrive from everywhere, it will rise from the waves, representing 'Liberty Enlightening the World.'"[17] Furthermore, all contributions, the appeal stated, would be gratefully accepted. "Let the number of signatures," read the appeal, "express the sentiments of France."[18]

It was originally estimated that the statue would cost about 240,000 francs, or 60,000 U.S. dollars. However, this estimate turned out to be much too low.

As might be expected, the liberal French press, which supported the government, was generally very enthusiastic about the idea to build America a monument to liberty. The conservative and monarchist newspa-

Despite criticism at home, Édouard-René Laboulaye pursued funding for the statue.

pers, still angry over the defeat of the plan to restore the monarchy to the throne, were generally very critical of the idea.

Laboulaye ignored their criticism. He was concentrating on securing American financial aid for the project. He wrote a letter to the editor of the American newspaper *Courrier des Etats-Unis*, which many French people living in the United States read. In it, he suggested that a similar committee to his Franco-American Union be established. Americans embraced the idea, and the new group was called the French Committee.

Meanwhile, the Franco-American Union was giving the impression that Bartholdi had made some type of arrangement while he was in the United States to have the Americans not only accept the statue but also to find a home for it. In reality, he

ULYSSES S. GRANT

Born Hiram Ulysses Grant in southwestern Ohio in 1822, Grant was a curious mixture of a man. He was a miserable failure in every business venture he tried early in life. However, when the American Civil War erupted in 1861, he reenlisted in the army and rose to commanding general after a string of spectacular military successes. He became the nation's eighteenth president in 1868, and he

Bartholdi spoke with President Grant (pictured) about the Statue of Liberty.

was the chief executive whom Bartholdi approached about the idea of the Statue of Liberty. A man of personal character, he had the unfortunate habit of implicitly trusting his friends, which got him into frequent trouble and caused his two administrations to be some of the most corrupt in American history. He died in 1885.

had done no such thing; he had acted instead like a public-relations agent, talking about the statue but never actually making any arrangements. He had spoken to American president Ulysses S. Grant about securing Bedloe's Island for the statue, but all Grant had told him was that congressional approval would be needed for that to happen. Finally, on October 26, 1875, Laboulaye presented a formal request to President Grant for Bedloe's Island to be the home of the statue.

A GOOD START

With money concerns for the statue uppermost in his mind, Laboulaye knew that he needed more money than donations would provide. Thus, on November 6, 1875, he held a huge formal fund-raising dinner at the Hôtel du Louvre in Paris. "Compared to our Statue," he said at the dinner, "the Colossus of Rhodes is but a clock ornament."[19] He also went on to explain that France would pay for the statue, and America would pay for the pedestal.

The dinner was a big success. It raised forty thousand francs for the project. Among the donors was Great Britain's largest manufacturer of gas lamps. The company pledged to provide—free of expense—the light that the statue was expected to use as a lighthouse.

The dinner also made a believer out of Ambassador Washburne. A naturally cautious man, Washburne had been uncertain whether this gigantic statue would ever be built. Previously he had forwarded the Bedloe's Island request to the U.S. State Department with no comments of his own, despite having pledged his total support for the project. He wanted to see what the statue looked like and what its chances of being built were before backing the project any further.

The banquet, and the model of the statue, produced a slightly more enthusiastic letter from Washburne to U.S. Secretary of State Hamilton Fish a few days later. "The project of erecting a monument seems to be taking on considerable proportions," Wash-

Bartholdi worked tirelessly on raising money to keep his statue alive.

burne wrote, "Although I have not myself felt certain of its success."[20] Washburne went on to halfheartedly endorse the project, pointing out how good it would be for French-American relations if it succeeded. Even still, U.S. government officials such as Washburne were ambivalent about the statue.

After the fund-raiser, contributions from France began pouring in to the Franco-American Union. Paris gave two thousand francs, and the cities of Le Havre and Rouen gave one thousand francs and five hundred, respectively.

Next the, Franco-American Union sent out fourteen financial subscription blanks all across France. They received contributions totaling about two hundred thousand francs from French men, women, and children from all walks of life.

FUND-RAISING EFFORTS

Although fund-raising started out on a positive note, the money that had been collected was being depleted to pay for the initial workers and their materials. In desperation the fund-raisers set up another event: a gala musical affair held at the Paris Opera on April 26, 1876. Composer Charles Gounod created a special composition, "Liberty Enlightening the World," for the occasion.

Unfortunately, the evening bombed. The regular operagoers were primarily wealthy, conservative supporters of the monarchists, and they did not approve of the idea of the statue, so they showed their displeasure by ignoring the event. Only four hundred people attended, and the evening itself produced just eight thousand francs.

Then help came from a most unexpected source: Bartholdi. In November 1875 he decided to sell the statue's copyright. This meant that he was selling the right to use the statue's image in advertisements and the like. It was a bold move by the sculptor, who did not know if the copyright would ever be worth anything. But the offer induced scores of French businessmen to sign up and pay for the right to use the statue's likeness in their advertising.

THE PHILADELPHIA CENTENNIAL EXPOSITION

The union decided early in 1876 that it should send something to the United States in honor of that nation's one hundredth birthday, even if the statue itself would not be ready. The union decided to send the arm holding the torch to the Philadelphia Centennial Exposition (similar to a world's fair, which showcased modern inventions and exhibits) in May 1876. It would be the first piece of the statue constructed.

Bartholdi, who had been appointed an adjunct commissioner to the exposition, began work on the right forearm and torch. Be-

THE PHILADELPHIA CENTENNIAL EXPOSITION OF 1876

Held in 1876 to celebrate America's one-hundredth birthday, the exposition was the model for future world's fairs, which were international expositions featuring exhibits and people from across the globe. The Philadelphia Centennial Exposition contained two sections, one on the Smithsonian Institution and one on the natural history of North America. The exposition was a great success, and many of the exhibits found their way to the Smithsonian in Washington, D.C.

cause it was just a small portion of the statue, he thought he would be able to finish it quickly. It was also relatively small—only about thirty feet in length—so he built it in his studio.

DOUBTS ABOUT THE STATUE

It was hoped that the arm and torch would rekindle America's enthusiasm for the statue, since an initial burst of excitement had been replaced by indifference. During the mid-1870s America's energies were focused on settling the western frontier and recovering from an economic slowdown that had begun in 1873, not on a giant statue.

In addition, there was a lot of resentment in America aimed toward New York. The city was considered the home of fat-cat industrialists and wealthy bankers—people who were viewed with disdain by many other Americans. The statue was seen not as an American gift celebrating liberty but as a gift to New York City.

U.S. government officials were also having doubts about the statue. Secretary of State Fish had written to Washburne that he doubted that France could make the proposed monument. Other government officials were worried about the cost of the ceremony in which the monument was to be accepted, raising the money to pay for the pedestal, and having the statue function as a lighthouse.

Some American newspaper editors found the notion of a statue dedicated to abstract concepts like liberty and freedom difficult to understand. For instance, the *New York Herald* suggested that Bartholdi should instead create a statue honoring

Workers in Bartholdi's studio complete a full-scale model of the statue's hand and part of the torch as curious visitors look on.

someone like Lafayette, the famous French hero of the American Revolution.

Despite the criticism, Bartholdi hoped that this was just a small backlash in the United States and that Americans would become thrilled about the statue all over again when they saw the arm and torch. However, his plan got off to a bad start. He could not complete the arm and torch in time for the start of the Philadelphia Centennial Exposition.

The arm and torch were still not ready by July 4, 1876, when they could have brought maximum publicity value, and so the sculptor was forced to rely on a canvas backdrop that had been painted for the opera event, showing how the statue would look in New York Harbor. Bartholdi unveiled the backdrop to the New York Club on July 4, uncertain of the club's reaction. To his great relief, the event received wide and favorable coverage in the New York newspapers.

EXCITEMENT BEGINS TO BUILD

The arm and torch finally arrived in America on August 14, 1876. It took twenty men to carry the packing crate containing the arm and torch ashore from the ship on which it had made its journey. It was set up outside, near the Hall of Machinery, at the exposition. There, it quickly became a major tourist attraction. For a fee, which went to the Franco-American Union, people could climb up the inside of the arm and emerge outside, on the torch. On one particular day, 125,000 people visited the arm and torch. Stories and articles about the arm and torch, and the statue itself, began appearing in newspapers all over the country.

On September 6, 1876, a statue of Lafayette, which French president Louis-Adolphe Thiers had commissioned Bartholdi to create to thank the people of New York City for their support during the Franco-Prussian War, was publicly unveiled. Bartholdi, on hand for the presentation, pulled the rope that removed the cover from his statue. As he did, the crowd began applauding and cannons fired a salute.

Bartholdi used this opportunity to talk about *Liberty Enlightening the World*. With praise for both statues ringing in his ears, Bartholdi organized a boat trip to Bedloe's Island for some New York officials. During the excursion he talked about how perfectly the statue would fit on the island. Bartholdi became the best promoter for his project. With great eloquence, he would speak to every club and organization he could, talking about how wonderful the statue would look standing in New York Harbor.

THE PHILADELPHIA STORY

But Bartholdi's efforts were not sufficient to stifle all criticism. When the *New York Times* of September 29, 1876, ran a harsh editorial about paying for the statue and the pedestal, Bartholdi wrote a furious reply, stating that if New York was going to be so stingy then he would place the statue in Philadelphia.

The basis for the *Times* story stemmed from the paper's suspicion that the French expected the Americans to pay for the entire statue, considering its ever-increasing cost. The paper also cast doubt on Bartholdi's motives for building the statue, saying that if the sculptor was serious about actually constructing it, he

Liberty's hand and torch dominate the skyline at the 1876 Centennial Exhibition in Philadelphia.

would not have only made the arm and torch to display, but rather he would have started from the ground up.

In reality, Bartholdi had no intention of placing his statue in Philadelphia; his threat was merely an effort to make New York think it might lose the statue to a rival city. The sculptor revealed his true feelings about the matter in a letter to Laboulaye. In it, he said that having the statue in Philadelphia would not be the same.

Bartholdi's ploy worked. An organization called the Harmony Club, which had been involved in the Lafayette statue project, formed a group called the Franco-American Union Statue of Liberty–New York Committee to muster support for the statue and raise money for the pedestal.

Bartholdi's Philadelphia strategy also caused the *New York Times* to change its opinion. The newspaper attacked Philadelphia for its act of "piracy," and it said that all Philadelphia could do was place the statue in the Delaware River, where it could guide fishermen and muskrats to their homes. The editorial also contained a stern warning about the city's potential for losing the statue if it did not raise the funds needed for the pedestal.

When the Philadelphia Centennial Exposition closed in November 1876 the arm and torch moved to Madison Square Park in New York City, at Fifth Avenue near Twenty-third Street. People paid fifty cents for the privilege of climbing up the arm and clambering out onto the balcony surrounding the torch.

It sat in the park for six long years—more of an oddity than a symbol of liberty. The *New York Times*, back to criticizing the statue, felt that this was only the first step in the plot to defraud America: "Other pieces . . . will be erected in the parks and squares of the city,"[21] wrote the paper. Many felt that the promise of the statue was just being used to trick Americans into paying for something that would never be built.

ANOTHER COMMITTEE

With fund-raising in France proceeding, some Americans realized that they had to get serious about raising money for the pedestal. Thus, in December 1876 another fund-raising group for the pedestal was formed: the American Committee for the Statue of Liberty. This one had many important people as members, including the poet William Cullen Byrant and William M. Evarts, who would be named secretary of state in the upcoming

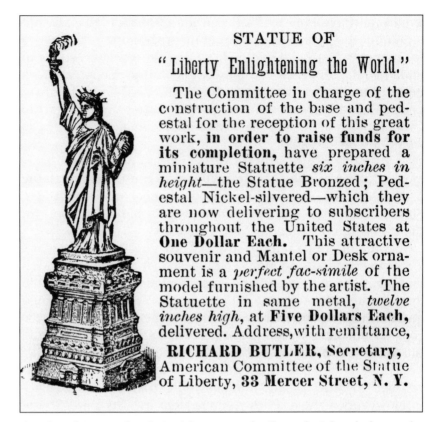

STATUE OF

"Liberty Enlightening the World."

The Committee in charge of the construction of the base and pedestal for the reception of this great work, **in order to raise funds for its completion,** have prepared a miniature Statuette *six inches in height*—the Statue Bronzed; Pedestal Nickel-silvered—which they are now delivering to subscribers throughout the United States at **One Dollar Each.** This attractive souvenir and Mantel or Desk ornament is a *perfect fac-simile* of the model furnished by the artist. The Statuette in same metal, *twelve inches high*, at **Five Dollars Each,** delivered. Address, with remittance,

RICHARD BUTLER, Secretary, American Committee of the Statue of Liberty, **33 Mercer Street, N. Y.**

An advertisement aimed at raising money for the pedestal seeks buyers for replicas of the statue.

administration of President Rutherford B. Hayes. The committee began trying to raise money for the statue's pedestal, which it estimated would cost $125,000.

The group also unveiled a painting called *Liberty Lighting the World's Commerce* by Edward Moran. It showed the statue in all its glory situated in New York Harbor, as ships from many nations gathered around it.

The committee also petitioned President Ulysses S. Grant for the right to place the statue either on Governors Island or Bedloe's Island in New York Harbor. (Nothing had come from Laboulaye's initial request.)

Evarts brought the resolution to the House and Senate, and he made sure that an important member of each major party (Democratic and Republican) introduced it so that it would have bipartisan support. The resolution passed both legislative chambers on February 22, 1877, without a single dissenting vote—undoubtedly helped by the fact that the French were paying for the statue and the pedestal was supposed to be paid for via private donations. Evarts then personally took the document to the White House and had Grant sign it on March 3, 1877, Grant's last full day in office.

MORE MONEY PROBLEMS

The reason the arm and torch sat in Madison Square Park for so long was that work on the statue was progressing slowly because of a lack of money. The estimated cost of the project kept rising—soon it went from 240,000 to 600,000 francs. It was simply very difficult to work on a statue that depended primarily on public subscriptions for funds.

The Franco-American Union kept trying to raise money, however. In August 1877 it produced a diorama (a three-dimensional scene produced by placing objects in front of a painted background) showing how the statue would look standing in New York Harbor. When Grant, the former American president, saw the diorama in November 1877 in the midst of a world tour, the event received a lot of favorable publicity.

Bartholdi helped as well by waiving his copyright fees on one hundred three-foot terra-cotta replicas of the statue that were sold to raise more money. They have been called the most accurate representations of the statue ever made. To ensure that they would become collector's items, Bartholdi destroyed the molds after the statues were produced. They were sold for one thousand francs in France and three hundred dollars in the United States. As a bonus, the buyer's name could be engraved into the model before it was placed into the furnace for baking.

Even still, not enough money was raised. In desperation Bartholdi contracted with a French firm, Avoiron et Cie, to produce four-foot-high copper-plated zinc models of the statue. But for reasons unknown, only six of these were made. (More copies were made of a two-foot-tall model.)

Bartholdi also arranged the production of a beautiful but inexpensive medal of the statue, which he personally gave to anyone he felt had performed services on the statue's behalf. This did not bring any money to the project, however.

In midsummer 1879 the Franco-American Union decided to hold a national lottery to raise the money needed for completion

Replicas of the statue, like this 1870 model, were sold for three hundred dollars apiece.

of the statue, which was then about two hundred thousand francs short. It contacted the French Ministry of the Interior for permission to conduct the lottery, and it persuaded companies throughout France to donate 538 prizes, including a four-thousand-dollar table service. The plan was to sell three hundred thousand tickets in both France and America, at the price of one franc each, or around twenty-five cents in U.S. dollars.

The lottery raised money slowly, and the final drawing had to be rescheduled from December 1879 to June 1880. But the union at last reached its goal. On July 7, 1880, more than five years after fund-raising had begun, the Franco-American Union announced that it had enough money. On that same day, the union held a formal "notification dinner" at a Paris hotel, informing the Americans that there were no longer any obstacles to completing the statue.

The American Committee, headed by Evarts, did not immediately respond to the news. When it did, it was in the form of a flowery letter from the committee chairman, assuring the Franco-American Union that the American Committee would raise enough money to build the statue's pedestal.

Unbeknownst to Bartholdi, flowery assurances were about all that he was going to receive from the Americans. In reality, fund-raising for the pedestal was going very slowly in America. Soon enough, he would learn about the pedestal problems. However, that was after he had built what would become one of the most beloved statues of all time.

Building a Dream

When enough money had been collected, Bartholdi began steady work on the statue. He did not build the statue from the ground up, but rather in pieces. He then assembled the statue outside because it was so large. At the same time, he had to worry about the internal skeleton, or support, for the statue. Viollet-le-Duc had died in 1879, and his unexpected death left Bartholdi dependent on a different engineer for the inside skeleton. But just as he had done with the fund-raising, Bartholdi managed to overcome all obstacles and build "his American."

Bartholdi on the Move

Building the Statue of Liberty required Bartholdi to perform many different tasks. Because of its size, the Statue of Liberty was built in sections. Each section was made to his precise specifications. All the sections fit together like a giant jigsaw puzzle. In addition, to send the statue to America would require that it be taken apart; no ship could fit a 151-foot-tall statue in its hold.

COPYRIGHT EFFORTS

During the construction of the statue, Bartholdi also took the time to register it with the U.S. Patent Office in Washington, D.C. This meant that anyone in the United States who produced copies of the statue in any form, including photographs, had to pay a copyright fee or royalties to Bartholdi. In theory, registering the statue should have guaranteed Bartholdi great profit since the statue soon became a popular item for American businesses to display in advertisements. Yet this was not the case. All Bartholdi could do was go to court to stop illegal displays or reproductions of the statue from being produced, and the companies that came to him to obtain legal permission to produce the statue were few and far between.

Craftsmen work on the head of the colossal statue in Bartholdi's workshop/warehouse.

As he ran from section to section, supervising the workmen, Bartholdi found time to arrange for the purchase and delivery of all required materials, tinker with the design, and publicize the progress he was making on the statue.

Bartholdi's Paris neighbor was the firm of Gaget, Gauthier, and Company, which had built several statues using the copper repoussé method, including a twenty-two-foot-high equestrian statue of the Gallic chief Vercingetorix. It had also worked with copper in creating the cupola of the Paris Opera and the statues of the famous cathedral of Notre Dame. Thus, the firm seemed like a logical choice to help build the statue. Sometime in the first part of 1877, Bartholdi engaged Gaget, Gauthier, and Company to help him build the statue.

BUILDING MODELS OF THE STATUE

Bartholdi began building one of the greatest monuments in history by constructing a finely detailed four-foot-high clay model

of the statue. Once he had perfected the model, he made a series of plaster models of the clay statue that were one-sixteenth
the size of the actual memorial. Next, he made another model
that was one-eighth the size of the original, and finally, another
that was one-quarter the size. At each
stage the sculptor refined the design,
smoothing out lines, wrinkles, and unnecessary details. He firmly believed
that a statue as big as the Statue of Liberty must not have any unnecessary
details that would distract from its
overall power and majestic effect.

To enlarge the model, workers first
marked hundreds of reference points
on contour lines drawn around the
model's surface. Then they geometri-
cally measured the height, depth, and
width of each point's location on two
separate frames, one above and one
around the model's base.

Next, Bartholdi broke down the
one-quarter-size model into 210 sections, and these sections became the
models for the final statue. He hung
each section inside a three-dimensional
framework—something like an open
square. He next hung a series of string
lines on each section, then took exact
measurements from the lines to the section. He covered each section with dots
that were used as measuring guides. As
the measurements were taken on the
first set of sections, they were enlarged
four times to the model being built in
the second set of sections. This is how
Bartholdi and his workmen built a plaster enlargement four times as large as
the first, or full size.

The measuring was work of the
highest precision. Each reference point
had to be measured six times—the

*A four-foot-high clay model, one of
many models built by Bartholdi.*

width, depth, and height on the model—then the same three dimensions for the full-size model. Each section of the statue had fifteen hundred reference points, for a total of nine thousand separate measurements on each section. If one measurement was incorrect, it could throw the entire statue off. Any mistake would also not be easy to hide; it would come out four times as large on the finished statue.

Next in the construction process came the duplication of the plaster model on the copper sheets. It took approximately 350 thin copper sheets to build the statue. However, since the copper sheets could not be hammered directly against the plaster because of the danger of shattering the material, the workmen first built large wooden molds, called garabits, that duplicated, in reverse, the many shapes, lines, and contours of the plaster's surface. This was done by having the workmen carve planks of wood and fit them directly against the full-size plaster model. Crosspieces of wood were inserted between the planks, forming pigeonholes. The more complicated the plaster surface, the more crosspieces of wood were inserted. Sometimes, enough crosspieces were inserted to form a solid wooden surface against which to beat the copper.

These wooden molds, called lattice molds, had to be built in sections when the statue's surface curved in deeply. This was done so they could be easily removed from the plaster model and also so the copper could be easily removed from the mold once it was hammered into shape.

Eventually an entire portion of the plaster model's surface was covered with these wooden molds. Once each mold was finished, it was pulled away from the plaster model and was laid on its back so the reverse copy of the statue's surface faced upward. Most often, a mold had to be hammered into a supporting device, called a cradle, to hold it firmly in place for the copper workers.

MOLDING THE COPPER

The statue required a large amount of copper to complete the project. Fortunately, the French industrialist Pierre-Eugène Secrétan donated 64 tons of copper for the project. It is speculated that the copper came from the Visnes Coppermines at Karm Island, a small rocky island off the southwestern coast of Norway. This French-owned mine was a significant source of northern

Workers build lattice molds that provided the shape and structure of the statue's hand.

European copper in the late nineteenth century. By 1895, 1.8 million tons of copper ore had been extracted from it.

Now it was the coppersmiths' turn to work on the statue. Each individual copper plate was pressed into its wooden mold with a large lever and held in place with vises and lead weights that were hung around the edge of the plate. Once the plate was properly situated, the coppersmiths hammered it with wooden mallets to precisely fit it to the contours of the mold. As they worked on a piece of copper, they would use smaller hammers with iron heads for finely detailed work. When complicated shapes or details were needed, the copper was heated first with a blowtorch to make it easier to hammer (heated metal is more easily bent) and also to keep it from cracking.

This method of building a statue was called the pointing-up method. A majority of the hammering and shaping was done on the inside of the plate. When done, a plate was turned over to reveal a smooth image on its outside surface. That image would be the one seen by the world.

However, before a piece of copper could be considered finished, workers had to make two-inch-wide iron straps to exactly fit the plate. These iron ribs were attached vertically and horizontally to the inside of each plate, to keep it from sagging.

When a copper plate was finished, it was brought outside and was hoisted up to the statue's supporting skeleton by means of ropes and pulleys. Once it was in place, workers would attach it with temporary screws. They did not want to permanently attach it because it would eventually be taken apart and shipped to America.

THE WORKSHOP

With all of this activity—coppersmiths hammering, carpenters cutting, plasterers constructing—Bartholdi's workshop was a busy place indeed. A reporter for the *New York World* reported the frantic scene in Bartholdi's workshop in 1878:

> The workshop was built wholly and solely for the accommodation of this one inmate and her attendants, some fifty workmen hammering for their lives on sheet copper to complete the toilet of her tresses for the show. The Lilliputians reached her back hair by means of ladders running from stage to stage on a high scaffolding. I mounted the scaffolding with them and stood on a level with her awful eye some thirty inches from corner to corner to be engulfed in her gaze. . . . The whole scene abounded in this curiosity of measurement. A number of pygmies of our species crawling about the inside of what appeared to be a vast cauldron used in the sugar refining trade were understood to be really at work on the crown of her head. A smaller cauldron, on which two little fellows were busy in a corner, was the tip of her classic nose. Her lips, from dimple to dimple, were as long as my walking stick, and fifteen people, I was told, might sit around the flame of her torch.[22]

As the reporter noted, the workshop was conducting several different activities simultaneously. Once the plasterers were done with one section, they moved on to the next section, and the carpenters began building their lattice molds. When the carpenters were done, they, too, moved on to the next section while the coppersmiths began hammering their copper plates. Meanwhile, the plasterers were starting on another section. Soon the workshop was filled with lattice molds, plaster models, and hammered pieces of copper.

Despite the vast amount of work being done, not every section of the statue was built in Bartholdi's workshop. Some sections were made in other parts of France; for example, one finger was fashioned by a coppersmith living in the southern part of the country. But wherever sections were made, each workman had to follow Bartholdi's very detailed instructions.

THE PARIS UNIVERSAL EXPOSITION

Even as he was building the statue, Bartholdi kept publicizing his efforts in order to keep the French public enthused about the project and to help the fund-raising efforts. In the summer of 1878 came another opportunity to put his statue in the news—the Paris Universal Exposition (another type of world's fair). For the exposition, the sculptor prepared the head and shoulders, which stood seventeen feet high. It was the second piece of the statue to be completed. It was brought to the exposition on a cart drawn by twelve horses.

As it made its way through the Paris streets, the statue swayed back and forth in the cart, giving the impression that the giant head was nodding as it went by the crowds of people that had gathered to watch its passing. When it was set up, about forty people could stand

The statue's head and shoulders are displayed at the 1878 Paris Universal Exposition.

in the observation room that Bartholdi had included inside the statue's head. The statue's exhibit at the Paris Universal Exposition renewed France's excitement about the project.

EIFFEL BUILDS THE INFRASTRUCTURE

While the statue itself was being built, the inner supports for the statue were also being constructed. However, Viollet-le-Duc, the architect who was going to stabilize the interior of the statue by filling it with sand, had died on September 17, 1879, without leaving plans for what he was going to do and how he was going to do it. To replace him, Bartholdi selected Alexandre-Gustave Eiffel, who would later go on to build the world-famous Eiffel Tower in Paris.

Eiffel was a perfect choice to replace Viollet-le-Duc. Like Bartholdi, Eiffel enjoyed building colossal projects. As he said, "There is in the colossal an attraction, a particular charm, to which the theories of ordinary art are hardly applicable. Does one suppose it is by their esthetic value that the Pyramids have struck man's imagination so strongly?"[23]

Bartholdi and Eiffel had to work very closely together to ensure that the framework would precisely fit the outer skin of copper. However, Eiffel rejected Viollet-le-Duc's idea to attach the copper plates to an iron frame and then weigh down the body of the statue by filling it hip-high with sand. Eiffel was acquiring a reputation as one of the most brilliant and innovative people of his age. His specialty was the creation of metallic structures, such as the railroad bridge at the city of Garabit and the Bon Marche department store in Paris, which were very light yet very sturdy.

For Bartholdi's statue, Eiffel constructed a central tower, or pylon, made of wrought-iron plates connected together to form four giant girders, each almost one hundred feet high. They were angled toward each other and connected by bracing struts. This effectively carried the statue's weight. For the upraised arm he built a similar, but smaller, structure. It is forty feet, seven inches long and swings up and out from the main pylon.

Next, Eiffel had to figure out how to connect the pylon to the copper skin yet have it be strong enough to hold the statue's weight and survive all the fury of nature. For this, Eiffel used 1,830 light iron bars that attached to the pylon and reached out to the skin.

ALEXANDRE-GUSTAVE EIFFEL

French structural engineer Eiffel designed the inner supports for the Statue of Liberty.

Alexandre-Gustave Eiffel, creator of the famous tower in Paris that bears his name, was born in 1832. He attended the Collège Sainte-Barbe, where he was initially trained as a chemist. He eventually shifted his focus to engineering. In fact, he designed a railway bridge in Bordeaux. It was so light, sturdy, and modern that it opened up a whole new world in engineering for him. He founded his own company and soon became known for his wrought-iron structures. Soon after he completed *Liberty Enlightening the World* for Bartholdi, he began building the Eiffel Tower, an early example of wrought-iron construction on a massive scale. He died in 1923.

However, Eiffel had no intention of attaching the iron bars directly to the skin. He understood that if iron and copper came into direct contact, a harmful interaction called galvanic action would be produced. Instead, he used 325 thin iron bars, called saddles, to line the inside of the skin and then attached them to the iron bars connected to the pylon. He insulated them from each other with a layer of asbestos and shellac. Thousands of rivets (small metal pieces driven through two objects to hold them together) had to be driven through the outer skin and saddles to hold them in place. Eiffel made certain they would be hard to see from the outside, though, so as not to spoil the effect of Bartholdi's statue.

Thus constructed, the iron bars act like springs, allowing the statue to expand, contract, bend, and pivot according to the dictates of nature. The iron bars give the mammoth statue an amazing degree of flexibility; they allow the statue to move slightly yet still remain attached to the central pylon. Each copper piece is supported by one or more flat iron bars and does not weigh down on the plates beneath it. Thus, the statue can survive nature's fury

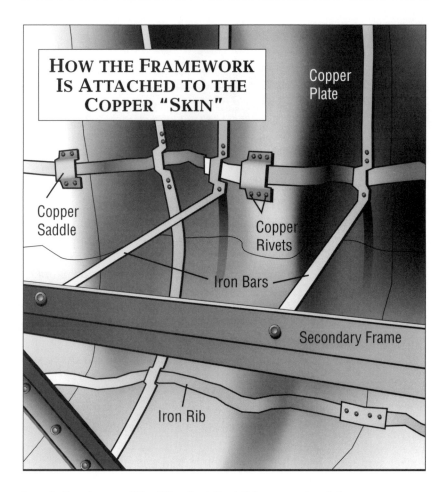

HOW THE FRAMEWORK IS ATTACHED TO THE COPPER "SKIN"

Copper Plate

Copper Saddle

Copper Rivets

Iron Bars

Secondary Frame

Iron Rib

in relative tranquility. The fact that it has survived for over a century is proof of the soundness and genius of Eiffel's design.

Inside the statue, a double spiral staircase winds around the center of Eiffel's pylon. Builders and guests could walk up one staircase and then exit via another. Each staircase contains 171 steps, roughly the same as a twelve-story climb. Resting stations were included along the way. It is not clear whether Bartholdi intended for tourists to climb inside his statue. But regardless, the staircases would soon be used for just that purpose.

Thus, three individual structural systems support the statue. The first is the main pylon, the second is the arrangement of iron that reaches out from the central pylon to the saddles, and the saddles themselves are the third system. The flat bars and secondary frame transfer the copper shell's weight back to the central pylon.

PUTTING THE PIECES TOGETHER

In October 1881 America and France celebrated the one hundredth anniversary of the Battle of Yorktown, which had been fought during the American Revolution and had been won by the combined forces of the two countries. To mark the occasion, Levi P. Morton, the new American ambassador to France, was asked to drive in the first rivet for the final assembly of the statue that would join all of the individual pieces together.

In the spring of 1881 workmen began to assemble the individual parts of the statue on the Rue de Chazelles, the street next to the workshop. Unlike the way the statue was built, the assembly was done from the ground up, starting with the feet. Scaffolding surrounded the statue, and, of course, Eiffel's armature had to be in place first to give the workmen something to

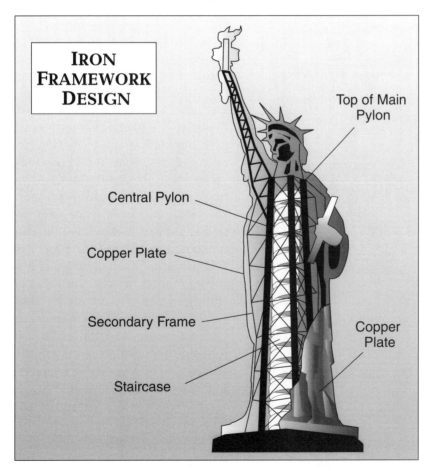

IRON FRAMEWORK DESIGN

Top of Main Pylon

Central Pylon

Copper Plate

Secondary Frame

Staircase

Copper Plate

which to attach the sections. Some pictures that have survived from this era show the statue peering out majestically over the rooftops as it slowly rises up above its Paris neighbors. It must have been a strange sight to see—the colossal Statue of Liberty looming above the other buildings. People would come by to watch the workmen build this impressive structure.

In July 1882 the sculptor invited newsmen to lunch inside the statue, which by now had been built up to the waist. The reporters climbed up a ladder to the statue's knee, where they enjoyed one of the most unusual lunches of their lives. One of the newsmen reported that "twenty men can comfortably lunch in the knee of this statue."[24]

Surrounded by scaffolding, the statue is assembled from the ground up.

ANOTHER DEATH

In the following months, the statue continued to be assembled. However, during the process another death struck the project. The statue had already survived one important death—that of Viollet-le-Duc, the first structural engineer. On May 25, 1883, Édouard-René Lefebvre de Laboulaye died at the age of seventy-one. It had been his vision, and his iron determination, that had guided the statue through so many obstacles, especially in fund-raising. Laboulaye would never see the statue for which he had risked so much completed, nor would he ever see the statue standing proudly in New York Harbor. Bartholdi lamented, "I would have been so gratified to see him sharing our satisfaction in the completion of the work to which he had shown such devotion."[25]

However, Bartholdi continued to work hard on the statue, but there was much to do before it would be ready to give to the

THE BATTLE OF YORKTOWN

Yorktown, in Virginia, was the decisive battle of the American Revolution. American and French troops besieged the British under Lieutenant General Charles Cornwallis for twenty days. A French fleet sealed the harbor. After trying to escape and failing, Cornwallis realized that his situation was hopeless and asked for terms of surrender. A British rescue force of seven thousand men went back to New York upon hearing of the surrender. The capitulation brought about the resignation of Lord Frederick North, the British prime minister, and brought more conciliatory leaders into office. It was the last major action of the war. It was the one hundredth anniversary of this battle that remotivated the Americans to fund the Statue of Liberty's pedestal.

The British acknowledge America's victory at Yorktown.

Americans. With Laboulaye's death, no one knew who would take his place as one of the guiding lights of the project.

AMERICA ACCEPTS THE STATUE

Upon Laboulaye's death, the French government, surprisingly, became more involved in the project. It informed U.S. Ambassador Morton that it intended to turn over the statue to the

American government on July 4, 1884. Bartholdi was likely to complete the statue sometime that June.

This put Morton into a quandary. The statue had begun as a gift from the French people to the American people. But now the French government was getting involved. As yet, there was no commitment by the American government to accept the statue, and the campaign to build a pedestal was in a state of confusion. Morton did not know what to do.

He wrote to his government for instructions. Four days before the proposed transfer, he received a wire authorizing him to act on behalf of the president of the United States and accept the statue.

Thus, on July 4, 1884, a ceremony formally transferred the giant copper statue from France to America. There were speeches and a luncheon, and Bartholdi led a group of officials up the winding staircase inside the statue. Using a goose-quill pen decorated with ribbons in the colors of both nations, a report of the proceedings was signed by everyone present.

A FRENCH STATUE

While Bartholdi was building the statue, some three hundred thousand people had visited the workshop of Gaget, Gauthier, and Company. It was certainly an impressive sight to see. The statue weighed 225 tons and towered 152 feet in the air. Bartholdi and Eiffel had achieved what many thought was impossible.

Now that the statue was officially an American, more people wanted to see it. The statue was supposed to be disassembled on August 20, but the date was pushed back to late December to accommodate all those who wished to see the statue before it left France. In fact, so many people wanted to view the statue that the transit company added extra cars to accommodate all of the visitors.

But it was clear that the statue would eventually be shipped to the United States. This knowledge, and the fact that Frenchmen were starting to regret that the statue had to go to America at all, led Americans living in Paris on September 1, 1884, to issue a public call via the newspapers for the creation of a replica of the statue to be built for France.

Bartholdi's one-quarter-size model was selected as the easiest way to build a copy of the statue. This model was so finely detailed that the construction went swiftly. In the spring of 1885,

Ambassador Morton presented this replica to the people of France. It was initially placed in United States Square in Paris.

Four years later the replica would be moved to a more scenic site on the Island of Swans, near where the Eiffel Tower would eventually be built. The replica's plaque, which expressed the sentiments of the Americans in France, read: "We revere the France of the past because her soldiers have enabled us to become a nation, and we love the France of today because she has joined us in the cause of free government."[26]

To America!

On New Year's Day 1885, Bartholdi decided that the statue was ready to be shipped to America. The statue was carefully taken apart and was packed into 214 boxes. Some of the boxes were comparatively light—weighing as little as 150 pounds. Some of the boxes, however, were quite heavy, weighing as much as 3 tons.

Each box was numbered and identified so that the statue could be put back together correctly when it was ready to be rebuilt in New York. Then the boxes were brought to the railroad station, where a seventy-car train waited to take them to the French warship *Isère* for the long journey to the United States. The boxes were loaded into the ship's hold in reverse order so that the first pieces needed for assembly in America were the first to be unloaded.

On May 21, 1885, more speeches were given and more ceremonies were held at the site of the *Isère* and her escort ship, the *Flore*. Then the two ships set off for America. On board one ship was Bartholdi, who accompanied the Statue of Liberty on the first few miles of her journey. Then he disembarked, and the statue sailed on alone to the United States and to an uncertain future.

LIBERTY COMES
TO AMERICA

While Bartholdi was hard at work on the statue in France, Americans were trying to come up with both a design and the funds for Lady Liberty's pedestal. The pedestal was ultimately designed by the world-famous architect Richard Morris Hunt, but a lack of enthusiasm by the American people seriously hampered fund-raising efforts. It was only through the timely intervention of *New York World* publisher Joseph Pulitzer that enough money was raised at all. Even with Pulitzer's assistance, the statue was greeted by a half-finished pedestal when it arrived in America. Despite the delays, the dedication day for the statue finally arrived, and Bartholdi became the toast of America.

Architect Richard Morris Hunt designed Lady Liberty's pedestal.

BARTHOLDI'S PEDESTAL IDEAS

In the spring of 1877 the American Committee, which was raising funds for the pedestal, sent one of its members to France to get Bartholdi's viewpoint on the subject. The sculptor was quite clear that he did not want a pedestal with a grandiose design that would detract from his statue. He gave the American representative some drawings reflecting his views.

Three years later he sent more drawings to the committee reflecting a different pedestal design. He assumed that efforts were under way in America to build the pedestal, similar to those he was putting forth in France to build the statue. In reality, nothing could be further from the truth. Despite his best efforts to publicize his statue, building a pedestal for it was met by yawning indifference from the American people.

By 1881 the Americans had done almost nothing about the pedestal. But then, the ceremonies commemorating the one hundredth anniversary of Yorktown renewed interest in the statue, and Evarts decided to see how far along Bartholdi had gotten. He went to Paris and was astonished to see the sculptor's progress. He knew that the American Committee had to act quickly or the whole project could collapse without a pedestal, and it would be the Americans' fault.

Bartholdi's pedestal sketch.

ENTER HUNT

The American Committee knew that with Bartholdi working continuously, the statue was virtually certain to be completed. Thus spurred to action, the committee decided on a $125,000 budget for the pedestal, a timetable in which to build it (nine months), and, most importantly, an architect. On December 6, 1881, the committee named Richard Morris Hunt as the architect for the project.

Hunt was one of America's foremost architects. He had studied in Paris, so he was familiar with French architecture. In fact, Hunt was the first American to graduate from the École des Beaux-Arts in Paris. He had made his reputation building houses for the rich, but he wanted to construct other things.

As soon as he was named the pedestal's architect, Hunt wrote to Bartholdi for technical information about the statue, along with a request for the sculptor's pedestal ideas. The sculptor replied quickly, sending back detailed drawings and calculations.

Hunt's original plan for the pedestal was based on these drawings. He proposed building a pedestal 114 feet high and slightly tapered. The American Committee asked him to redo the design to cut down on the use of expensive granite. Therefore, Hunt reduced the pedestal height to 89 feet and kept it tapered at the top. He submitted his revised design on July 31,

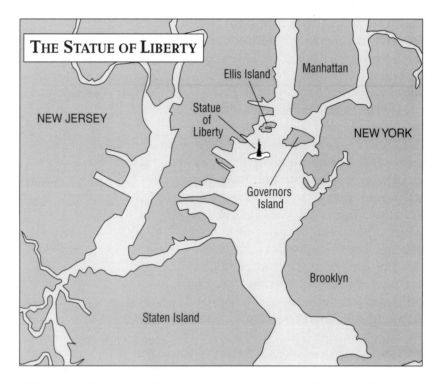

1884, and the committee accepted it one week later. The final design called for the pedestal to be 8,281 square feet at the bottom and 4,225 square feet at the top. The ground-level sides were 91 feet long, and the top sides were 65 feet long.

During the three years it took Hunt to design the pedestal, Bartholdi was becoming increasingly worried about the pedestal's slow pace and the problems the Americans were having raising money for it. On Halloween 1882 he wrote to the American Committee about his concerns. But at that time, the Americans could not allay his worries.

Finally, in November 1882, the American Committee held a large mass meeting at which it revealed its budget for the pedestal and other details. Many in the audience were shocked that the cost of the project had doubled from $125,000 to $250,000. Evarts eased the news somewhat by promising that as much as one-fifth of the money would be contributed by members of the committee.

Indeed, the members of the committee donated a lot of money, including Joseph W. Drexel, who gave five thousand dollars. Their contributions put some of the other wealthy men in the country to shame, such as John Jacob Astor, who gave twenty-five hundred dollars, and Andrew Carnegie, who contributed a mere five hundred dollars.

The indifference of America's wealthy illustrated the plight of the committee in raising money. Desperate for fund-raising ideas, the American Committee published a pamphlet entitled "An Appeal to the People of the United States in Behalf of the Great Statue of Liberty Enlightening the World." The pamphlet explained why cities all over the country should form subcommittees to promote the statue, and why they should not consider Lady Liberty just a New York City gift. They also sent a man named Mahlon Chance around the western United States on a fund-raising drive.

CONSTRUCTION BEGINS ON THE PEDESTAL FOUNDATION

Both of these fund-raising ideas flopped, however, and by the beginning of 1883 the committee's anxiety over the pedestal's construction increased. Thus, even though Hunt was still fiddling with the design and the pedestal had yet to be approved, and even though the committee was woefully short of money, it began laying the pedestal's foundation in April 1883. The committee hired General Charles Pomeroy Stone, who was on leave from the U.S. Army, to oversee the construction.

Stone plunged into the task, and soon Bedloe's Island was alive with construction activity. However, construction was more difficult than expected. It was discovered that Fort Wood (a fort built there during the Civil War) actually stood on top of sturdy masonry fortifications previously built by the Dutch. Stone could not build on top of these fortifications since the ground was primarily sand and was unlikely to support the foundation's weight. So he began digging.

After six months the excavation, which was 53 feet deep, was complete. Next the workers—mostly Italian immigrants who lived on Bedloe's Island during the winter—filled the giant hole with layer upon layer of concrete to provide a firm base for the statue. It took 24,000 barrels of cement and approximately nine months to lay the foundation, which became the largest concrete block in existence at the time. The dimensions of the foundation were almost as impressive as the statue itself. It weighed 23,500 tons and measured 91 square feet at the bottom and 65 square feet at the top. It rose upward to a height of 52 feet, 10 inches. Once the statue was placed on the pedestal, it would rise to nearly 305 feet high.

The foundation's construction also took virtually every penny collected by the American Committee. Meanwhile, other cities, such as Baltimore, San Francisco, and Washington, D.C., had expressed interest in having the statue placed in their city if New York could not raise the money for the pedestal.

The American Committee was desperate. It was out of money and out of ideas. It had sponsored art fairs and lecture tours and had sold miniature copies of the statue and three thousand copies of Bartholdi's autograph. It had even tried sending special solicitors into New York City's factories and office buildings begging for cash. However, nothing seemed to work.

The group known as the Sons of the American Revolution even pitched in by running a special steamboat line to Bedloe's Island, publicizing it with a big rally in the heart of New York City's financial district. But the results of the rally proved disappointing, yielding only about two thousand dollars.

Although the committee was desperate, it was not willing to accept money from just anybody. When a company offered to do-

Workers assembling Liberty's pedestal take a break.

nate $25,000 to the pedestal fund if it could place the name of its product—Castoria—across the top of the pedestal for one year, the committee declined. It did not want to taint Lady Liberty's image.

GOVERNMENT FAILURE

As a last resort the American Committee tried soliciting funds from several government bodies. It approached both New York City and the state, and it actually got an appropriation of fifty thousand dollars passed by both houses of the New York state legislature. But Governor Grover Cleveland vetoed it on the grounds that it was unconstitutional for any municipality to spend public funds on private matters.

The committee then appealed to the federal government, and it successfully persuaded both houses of Congress to include one hundred thousand dollars for the pedestal as part of an appropriations bill. President Chester A. Arthur favored spending the money. But when both houses of Congress tried to work out the differences between the two bills, the appropriation for the statue was inexplicably dropped.

Even reasonable ideas for raising money brought no response. When the *New York Times* suggested that each state contribute a sum for the honor of having its emblem engraved on the forty round, blank medallions (one for each state admitted to the Union) that were going to surround the statue, the states did not support the idea.

By March 1885 the American Committee had less than three thousand dollars in the bank. The blocks of granite that were needed for the pedestal, which came from Leeds Island, Connecticut, lay idly on the docks. There was no money to ship them to Bedloe's Island, nor was there any money to pay workmen to assemble them in the proper place. Construction ground to a halt on March 10. No one knew if it would ever start again.

PULITZER TO THE RESCUE

Just when it was darkest for the American Committee, Joseph Pulitzer entered the scene. Pulitzer was the publisher of the *New York World* newspaper. A Hungarian, German-speaking immigrant, Pulitzer fought with the Union army during the Civil War. After the war, he settled in St. Louis, where he bought the *St. Louis Dispatch* newspaper, merged it with the *St. Louis Post,* and turned it into a profitable and respected newspaper.

THE BARTHOLDI STATUE.
Even Liberty demands something substantial to stand upon.

An 1884 Thomas Nast cartoon urges the public to contribute money for the statue's pedestal.

In 1883 he bought the *New York World* from Jay Gould and transformed it into a newspaper of the people that always took the side of the "little guy" and rallied against big companies, rich people, and monopolies.

Pulitzer loved causes, and in the Statue of Liberty's pedestal he found a good one. He was outraged that, in a city known for its wealth and prosperity, the $250,000 could not be raised. He wrote,

> Here in the commercial metropolis of the Western world, where hundreds of our citizens reckon their wealth by millions, where our merchants and bankers and brokers are spoken of as "princes," we stand haggling and begging and scheming in order to raise enough money to procure a pedestal on which to place the statue.[27]

In March 1885, when work at Bedloe's Island ceased because of a lack of money, Pulitzer could barely control his anger:

> It would be an irrevocable disgrace to New York City and the American republic to have France send us this splendid gift without our having provided even so much as a landing place for it. There is but one thing that can be done. We must raise the money. The *World* is the people's paper, and it now appeals to the people to come forward and raise the money. Let us not wait for the millionaires to give this money. It is not a gift from the millionaires of France to the millionaires of America, but a gift of the whole people of France to the whole people of America. Take this appeal to yourself personally. . . . Give something, however little. . . . Let us hear from the people.[28]

The effect was immediate. Pulitzer had promised to print the names of everyone who made a donation, and he did this under a picture of Uncle Sam holding out his hat as if he were begging. The thrill of seeing one's name in the paper kept the donations coming in at a steady pace. In just two months the *World* raised $52,203, or more than a quarter of what it took the American Committee seven years to raise.

People sent in whatever amount they could afford, no matter how little. A woman named Jane sent in fifty cents. The twelve public schools of Trenton, New Jersey, sent in $105.07. After former president Ulysses S. Grant died in July 1885, a group of readers wrote in to say that they had walked home from the funeral service so they could donate their fifty-cent streetcar fare

JOSEPH PULITZER

Through public donations, Pulitzer successfully raised the money needed to erect Liberty's pedestal.

Born in 1847 in Hungary, Pulitzer came to America in 1864 and fought on the side of the Union during the Civil War. In 1869 he was elected to the Missouri House of Representatives. After leaving politics, he ventured into business. In 1878 he bought the *St. Louis Post* and also the *Evening Dispatch* and combined them into one newspaper. By 1883 he had acquired the *New York World* newspaper and turned it into one of the leading newspapers in the nation. Pulitzer introduced such newspaper staples as the comics, sports pages, and a woman's fashion section. He also focused on politics and controversial subjects. In fact, competition between the newspapers of Pulitzer and William Randolph Hearst was fierce during the Spanish-American War. Pulitzer died in 1911.

to the fund. Eighty percent of the total donations was received in sums of less than one dollar.

Many immigrants contributed. Some had seen enough of monarchical governments to appreciate liberty, and others were grateful to be in America and felt it was their duty to give something back to the country. Some of their ancestors had fought in the American Revolution, alongside Lafayette, and wanted to express their appreciation to the French. A few readers even sent in their contributions in Confederate money.

Pulitzer's determination to print letters from the contributors helped immensely in the fund drive. One such letter read, "I have lost 25 pounds and I am happily sending in a penny per pound. May heaven help you in your good work. It seems that New York's rich men do not."[29]

Pulitzer had placed veteran reporter John R. Reavis in charge of the fund-raising effort. As the total collected mounted higher, Reavis wrote to Pulitzer, "I am glad of my success not only for my sake but for your sake, the paper's sake, and the sake of the country. It is a grand thing to see a newspaper leading the sentiment of a nation."[30]

Since the *World* was one of the most influential newspapers in the country, its campaign for pedestal contributions had an effect across the rest of the United States. Donations were pledged from Iowa, Florida, California, Colorado, Missouri, and other states. It even received contributions from other countries, such as Ireland, Scotland, Italy, and Cuba.

Even other newspapers in other cities became enthusiastic supporters of the fund drive. Papers from Pittsburgh, Cleveland, Boston, Philadelphia, St. Louis, and Cincinnati, among others, ran stories and editorials praising the *World*'s effort and urging their readers to help. The crusade to build a pedestal, once solely thought of as a New York fight, was becoming nationwide in scope.

WORK BEGINS AGAIN

Work finally resumed at Bedloe's Island. When the statue arrived on June 17, 1886, most of the one hundred thousand dollars that was still needed for the pedestal had been collected by the *World*. Pulitzer and his readers had saved the Statue of Liberty. "The people have done their work well," Pulitzer wrote. "Their liberality has saved the great Republic from disgrace."[31]

The World *newspaper's lead story on August 11, 1885, proudly proclaimed victory in the collection effort.*

It was true. By August a little over one hundred thousand dollars had been collected. "One Hundred Thousand Dollars!" announced the *World* in large type on the front page. The drawing of Uncle Sam with hat in hand was replaced by one showing him completing an inscription on a pedestal: "This Pedestal of LIBERTY was provided by the Voluntary Contributions of 120,000 PATRIOTIC CITIZENS of the American Union through the NEW YORK WORLD. *Finis Coronat Opus*"[32] (meaning "The end crowns the work").

Pulitzer turned over one hundred thousand dollars to the pedestal committee, and he spent the remainder on a silver globe trophy atop a polished wooden base, which was created by Tiffany's and was presented to Bartholdi.

Bedloe's Island became a beehive of activity. Derricks worked furiously to lift the Connecticut stones of the pedestal into place. Because the statue had already arrived, workmen raced about the island, trying to get everything ready. They quickly finished the pedestal and it was finally ready for the statue.

ARRIVAL OF THE STATUE

When the statue actually arrived on June 17, 1886, it was greeted with pomp and pageantry. Representatives of the federal, state, and municipal governments went out to greet the French ships. A naval squadron escorted the ships through the harbor, and salutes were fired by naval guns.

Crowds estimated at two hundred thousand people gathered on the waterfront to watch the *Isère* and its historic cargo. French and American flags flew from buildings. A parade wound its way through the city. The mayor of New York City delivered a stirring welcoming speech.

Two days after the ships arrived in New York Harbor, on June 19, 1886, another massive celebration honored the arrival of the statue. The mayor of New York City and other dignitaries clambered aboard four American naval ships and made the trip out to Bedloe's Island, where more speeches were made accepting the statue. Flags and pennants fluttered in the breeze. Band music played. Cannons roared in salute. Crowds cheered from the Battery, where they had gathered to watch the spectacle. When they were finished, the officials rode up Broadway to a grand reception at New York's City Hall.

PUTTING LIBERTY TOGETHER

But the work was not yet complete on Bedloe's Island. In addition to the money raised to complete the pedestal, more money was needed to reassemble the statue and Eiffel's supporting framework. This cost was pegged at between fifteen thousand and twenty thousand dollars.

General Stone gave an interview to the newspapers, asking that one or more wealthy persons give the money out of national pride. But nobody felt civic-minded enough to contribute.

Bartholdi, always trying to help, wrote to the committee that the money might be raised "by borrowing the amount from some banker and giving a mortgage upon the product of the entrance fee."[33] It was the sculptor's idea to charge twenty-five cents on

EMMA LAZARUS

As a young Jew, Emma Lazarus was indifferent to the persecution of European Jews until 1879, when a wave of anti-Jewish violence swept over Russia and eastern Europe. Awakened to the plight of her people, the young writer of some fame was asked by William Evarts to write something to be included in a literary auction that his committee was holding to raise money for the Statue of Liberty's pedestal. Her work, entitled "The New Colossus," has become almost as well known as the statue, although it was initially ignored when first produced. She died of cancer in 1887 at the age of thirty-eight.

The eloquent words of Emma Lazarus are engraved on the statue's base.

The New Colossus
Not like the brazen giant of Greek fame,
With conquering limbs astride from land to land;
Here at our sea-washed, sunset gates shall stand,
A mighty woman with a torch, whose flame
Is the imprisoned lightning, and her name
Mother of Exiles. From her beacon-hand
Glows world-wide welcome; her mild eyes command
The air-bridged harbor that twin cities frame.

"Keep, ancient lands, your storied pomp!" cries she
With silent lips. "Give me your tired, your poor,
Your huddled masses yearning to breathe free,
The wretched refuse of your teeming shore.
Send these, the homeless, tempest-tost to me.
I lift my lamp beside the golden door!"

weekdays and ten cents on Sundays for visiting the statue. If that was not acceptable, Bartholdi volunteered to come to America and go on a lecture tour.

Both ideas were rejected in favor of going to the federal government once again. By now the president was Grover Cleveland—the same man who had once vetoed a bill as New York's governor to give the American Committee money. But this time Cleveland sent Congress a special message asking for cash both to put the statue together and for the dedication ceremony. Eventually $56,500 was appropriated for both purposes.

The money was not appropriated without a battle, however. Representative Richard Bland of Missouri led the fight against giving any money. "We have no authority to waste the public funds to provide for an inauguration and good time for the citizens of New York,"[34] Bland argued. However, after much debate, the appropriation was agreed upon.

President Grover Cleveland asked Congress to appropriate money for erecting and dedicating the Statue of Liberty.

At last construction could proceed. When the first two copper plates were ready to be fastened to the iron strapping, Bartholdi's name was engraved on the first rivet and Pulitzer's name on the second. When the last rivet was in place, the statue loomed nearly 306 feet from sea level to torch. The Statue of Liberty was the world's tallest man-made structure.

Stone devised the statue's connection to the pedestal. He placed four gigantic steel beams at the bottom of the pedestal walls and four more at the top. The bottom beams were placed twenty-nine feet from the bottom of the pedestal. The statue's iron framework was attached to the top set of beams with great bolts measuring five and a half inches in diameter.

Both sets of beams were connected by steel girders running up along the inside of the walls. The beams were then attached to the pylon with large bolts. It has been said that the statue's attachment is so secure that before it could tip over, the entire island would have to be overturned.

Overall, reassembly of the statue took six hundred thousand rivets. When workers could not fit the original pieces together exactly, they drilled new rivet holes. Unfortunately, this left thousands of unused rivet holes in Lady Liberty, and allowed moisture to seep into the statue.

LIGHTING PROBLEMS

In addition to all of the financial problems encountered, one other event proved difficult for the statue: the notion that it was supposed to be a lighthouse. Originally, Bartholdi had envisioned one set of lights in the crown, with another set in the torch. Next, he thought that lights should be set up around the torch. Reflectors could be used to direct this light skyward, which he hoped would be seen for miles.

By the time the statue was nearing dedication, electric lights were replacing gas ones, and a whole new set of problems, such as where the power

Workers hurry to complete assembly of the statue on Bedloe's Island.

could be obtained for the lights, presented themselves. Edward H. Goff, president of the American Electric Manufacturing Company, said he would donate a power plant for Bedloe's Island capable of running twenty lamps of six thousand candlepower. He also offered to donate the lamps, wiring, and other necessary electrical accessories. It was estimated that this gift was worth about seven thousand dollars.

The American Committee also made arrangements with E. P. Hampson and Company to furnish electrical power for the first week that the statue was in operation, assuming that the U.S. government would then take over the lighting bill.

It was a lot to assume. The trouble began about a week before the dedication, when Lieutenant John Mills, an electrical expert with the U.S. Army, rendered a negative opinion about the plan to direct the light toward the sky. Mills thought that directing the light upward would confuse navigators because it would bounce off the clouds. He decided that moving the lights inside the torch would be better. He also put two rows of windows in the torch so the light would shine out onto the water.

Bartholdi protested that the intense heat generated by the lights would ruin the copper of the flame, and he was also uncertain how much illumination such a setup would provide. But he was ignored.

Things went from bad to worse when E. P. Hampson and Company could find no one to authorize the U.S. government to begin paying for the statue's electricity. E. P. Hampson finally agreed to donate the electricity until November 6, when the French delegation that had arrived at Bedloe's Island for the dedication ceremony left for home.

If the idea of putting lights inside the torch did not work, no one seemed to know how to make the statue emit enough light to function as a lighthouse. Mills wrote to Bartholdi for suggestions, but all that the sculptor could suggest was to cover the torch in some type of reflective metal, like gold, off of which light could reflect more easily.

DEDICATION DAY

Despite the lighting difficulties, the American Committee proposed September 3, 1886, as the official inauguration date of the statue. That date was eventually changed to October 28, possibly at the urging of Bartholdi, who pointed out that the summer in New York was very hot, and the weather was more pleasant in the autumn.

When the big day arrived, New York City spared no expense to put on a grand celebration. An official holiday was declared, flags and banners of both American and French colors were flying everywhere, and a parade of twenty thousand marchers wound its way through the city. Even President Cleveland was present for the celebration.

According to the *New York Times*, as the parade passed by Wall Street, office boys leaned out of windows and unspooled reams of ticker tape. Soon the air was thick with the material. This was the birth of the famous ticker-tape parade.

According to a persistent legend, Monsieur Gaget came to the dedication ceremonies, bringing along three trunks filled with miniature statue replicas. As the popularity of the replicas grew in America, so did a variation of his name—*gadget*.

The only thing that did not cooperate was the weather. It had rained the night before, and October 28 dawned gray, with a thick blanket of fog that virtually obscured the statue from all but the closest spectators.

However, on Bedloe's Island crowds of dignitaries swarmed around, waiting for the speech-making that was a hallmark of that era. Bartholdi himself was hiding in the head of the statue, and it was arranged that a man on the ground would wave to him when Evarts had finished his speech. Then the sculptor was supposed to pull the cord that released a giant French flag that was hiding the face of the statue, thus revealing Lady Liberty's face to everyone.

Unfortunately, at one point in his speech Evarts paused long for dramatic effect. Bartholdi's man on the ground thought the speech was over and frantically gave the signal. The flag then fluttered down, and the statue's face was revealed. An awesome noise arose from the crowds on shore, the boats sailing in the

An invitation to the 1886 dedication of the Statue of Liberty, one of the many invitations sent to dignitaries worldwide.

THE LADIES OF THE HARBOR

On the day the Statue of Liberty was dedicated, cruising in the harbor was a rather unique ship. It contained only women—members of the New York State Woman Suffrage Association. Except for Bartholdi's wife and one other woman, women had been barred from Bedloe's Island for the day because their safety could not be guaranteed. The irony of liberty being portrayed as a woman while women were not allowed at the statue's dedication was lost on inauguration officials. So the suffrage association chartered its own boat and cruised as close to the island as possible, protesting the exclusion of women from the island and also speaking out in favor of a woman's right to vote.

harbor, and those manning cannon—sirens, bells, cannon fire, and cheers all exploding in a symphony of noise. The Statue of Liberty had officially been unveiled. The dream of a few men to make a gift for America had become a reality.

After that, President Cleveland and a few other speakers made some remarks, but they were anticlimatic. Earlier the president had issued a proclamation naming this day as Bartholdi Day, saying to Bartholdi, "You are the greatest man in America today."[35] Now the proud sculptor received the accolades that he so richly deserved.

A gigantic fireworks show had been planned as a stirring conclusion to the day's events, but the weather made it impossible. That night, at a grand banquet given in honor of the French delegation that had been present for the statue's unveiling, there was supposed to be no wine, in deference to the powerful temperance movement. A Frenchman living in America at the time heard this and was shocked. He ordered and paid for the wine personally. He was later elected to the French Legion of Honor for his kindness.

Besides the weather, the only thing that marred the dedication program was the attempt to illuminate the statue so that it could perform its lighthouse function. When the system was turned on on the night of the dedication, a feeble light shone forth—far too dim to be useful as a lighthouse. Someone said that it looked like a glowworm.

When dedication day was finally over, the statue stood in New York Harbor, gazing out at the water and ships with unblinking eyes. *Liberty Enlightening the World* would soon be transformed from a mere statue into an American icon.

LADY LIBERTY: DECLINE AND RESTORATION

Over the past century or so, the statue has been the site of explosions and protests, it has been used in countless advertising and promotional campaigns, and it has been refurbished and modernized. Ironically, even though the Statue of Liberty had long been a beloved symbol of American values, it suffered from years of neglect, which culminated in a massive overhaul in the 1980s. Throughout it all the statue has remained as unchanging as the concept that it represents: liberty.

THE SYMBOL OF ARRIVAL

Back when Bedloe's Island was chosen as the site for the Statue of Liberty, little did Bartholdi and others know how appropriate the site would be. Within a few years, the statue would witness the beginning of one of the greatest waves of immigration in human history. In fact, over 17 million people came to America through Ellis Island (the nation's primary immigration station directly across from the Statue of Liberty) between 1897 and 1954.

The statue had a profound effect on these travelers from other lands. It meant they had finally arrived in America and the

ELLIS ISLAND

Originally called Oyster Island and then Gibbet Island, Ellis Island (named after a New York merchant) was initially a federal arsenal. In 1892 officials decided that Castle Garden, the immigration station in Manhattan, could no longer handle the flood of people and made Ellis Island the new station. Approximately 17 million people entered the United States through Ellis Island before it closed in 1954. In 1990 the former main building was reopened as an immigration museum after being restored.

chance they had taken in leaving the Old World for the New had succeeded. As one immigrant later recalled, "Seeing the Statue of Liberty was the greatest thing I've ever seen. It was really something. . . . To know you're in this country."[36]

Even though immigration laws have changed over the years and the flood of immigrants has been reduced to a trickle, the Statue of Liberty is still the first thing that immigrants see when they enter the United States via New York Harbor. It is the symbol of arrival. The statue is so closely associated with arriving immigrants that in 1972 the American Museum of Immigration opened at the bottom of its pedestal. (It was closed when the Ellis Island Immigration Museum opened in 1990.)

Even though the Statue of Liberty became a symbol to immigrants, it really did not become a symbol of America until World War I. It was during this conflict that the statue replaced the female figure of Columbia that had long represented the United States. So-called liberty loan drives encouraged Americans to buy war bonds, and the statue was used as a symbol for those drives.

An illustration by Frank Leslie shows immigrants entering New York Harbor, welcomed by the Statue of Liberty.

During World War II the statue again became synonymous with America. As *Life* magazine wrote,

> Never before has the Statue of Liberty seemed so important. Never before have so many millions dreamed of her overseas or so many Americans . . . traveled to Bedloe's Island somehow to absorb her perishable significance from the folds of her imperishable bronze.[37]

EXPLOSIONS ROCK THE STATUE

Besides serving as a focal point of immigration, the statue has been affected by a couple of nearby explosions. In 1911, twenty-five tons of dynamite accidentally exploded on a nearby Jersey City pier. The statue suffered a few broken windows and shattered lightbulbs.

On July 30, 1916, the Black Tom munitions dump, a small piece of land across the water near Jersey City, exploded in what was later found to be espionage by German agents. The shock waves were felt fifty miles south. Approximately one hundred rivets from the Statue of Liberty popped loose from their fittings, primarily in the right arm. Some shrapnel and debris also nicked the statue. It was closed for ten days while repairs were made.

In 1917 the arm holding the torch was closed, giving rise to the story that the Black Tom explosion had weakened it. In actuality, it was closed because the platform around the torch could only hold twelve sightseers at one time, and congestion was becoming a huge problem. Those with special permission could still climb the arm. After this, visitors had to be content with climbing to the crown, where they could look out twenty-five windows and see a spectacular view of New York Harbor.

PROTESTS

Because the statue signifies individual freedom, many protestors and demonstrators have used it as the site of their protests. One of the first political protests held at the statue occurred when protestors from the World War Veterans Wines and Beer League climbed to the crown and unfurled black mourning banners from the windows to protest their loss of liberty to drink during Prohibition.

Political protests at the statue became heated during the mid-1950s. In late 1956, soon after tanks from the Soviet Union crushed an anti-Communist uprising in Hungary, a Hungarian

Women demonstrate support for the Equal Rights Amendment in 1970 at the base of the Statue of Liberty.

man made his way to the torch and hung out both a Hungarian and an American flag.

The following year rebels supporting Fidel Castro's grab for power in Cuba used the statue for a demonstration. After Castro was in power, groups of anti-Castro protestors had their turn using the statue to demonstrate against his regime.

The Vietnam War was a polarizing event for the United States, and it was inevitable that the statue would be dragged into the middle of pro-war and anti-war demonstrations. In late December 1971 fifteen Vietnam veterans hung an American flag upside down from the crown to protest the war. This traditional and well-known distress signal was their way of demanding that the United States leave Vietnam.

In 1980 two Americans protesting the imprisonment of Elmer Pratt, a black radical in California, used suction cups to climb halfway up the statue and unfurl a banner demanding the release of Pratt. Ironically, it was this climb that eventually led to the closing of the Statue of Liberty for major structural repairs.

These protests, and others like them, illustrated the statue's importance in American culture. It represented the American ideal of liberty and justice for all. Thus, groups felt it was important to have the statue in their protests because it was a nonpartisan symbol of equality.

THE OLD SWITCHEROO

Throughout the years the statue has also faced changes in the people and agencies that administered it.

One autumn day in 1894 a reporter for the *New York Herald* came to Bedloe's Island to see how the Statue of Liberty was getting along. He found soldiers (the army still controlled the

BLACK TOM

One of the worst terrorist attacks in the United States occurred in July 1916 at Black Tom, a twenty-five-acre promontory jutting out from the New Jersey shoreline. Despite America's initial neutrality, Black Tom was an arsenal for weapons to be sent to Great Britain and France during World War I. The Germans, understandably concerned, responded by setting an explosion on the poorly guarded island. The blast triggered a chain reaction of explosions that reduced the property to smoking rubble. The blasts were heard fifty miles south. The total damage was $25 million.

entire island, except where the statue was located) casually fishing off a pier, an army mule peacefully eating grass, and a bar and restaurant. The masonry between the stones of the pedestal was covered in graffiti.

There was one lone guard or caretaker, a man hired by the former American Committee, which was now called the Citizens' Committee. The committee operated the ferries that traveled to the statue from New York City and used the profits to set up a beautification fund for minor statue repairs and pay for the caretaker. It was a casual effort, however. Because the army just cared about its own property, and because the federal Lighthouse Board was only concerned with the maintenance of the light as a lighthouse, the statue itself was essentially neglected.

Bartholdi visited the statue on a pleasure trip to America in the autumn of 1893 and was shocked at the ramshackle condition of Bedloe's Island. In an attempt to rally support for better maintenance of the island, he said,

Liberty Island [as he called it] is obviously destined to be made into a pleasure ground for the soul of the

Demonstrators protest U.S. government policies in Puerto Rico by hanging flags from the statue's crown.

American people, a place of pilgrimage for citizens of the whole nation, a National museum of the glories and memories of the United States.[38]

Bartholdi's eloquent words fell on deaf ears, however. The island continued to be neglected.

In the following years, many different organizations were responsible for the statue's maintenance. In 1902 the War Department officially became the custodian of the statue. The Lighthouse Board ended its haphazard maintenance of the Statue of Liberty. It was not until 1924 that President Calvin Coolidge proclaimed the Statue of Liberty a national monument. Nine years later the statue was put under the jurisdiction of the newly created National Park Service, where it remains to this day.

LIGHTING FIXES

Perhaps no part of the Statue of Liberty has received more attention and caused more problems than the lighting system. In the spring of 1887 the U.S. Lighthouse Board, under whose authority the statue fell, announced that it would use a new powerful lens, just like that used in new lighthouses, inside the Statue of Liberty. But when the board admitted that the new lens was "intended more to enhance the grandeur of the statue than as an aid to navigation,"[39] it was admitting that even installing this new lens would not hide the fact that the Statue of Liberty was a failure as a lighthouse. No one could figure out where to put lights or how to have them shine brightly enough to be seen far out to sea as a navigation aid. At one point even painting the statue white was considered as a way of improving its ability to reflect light!

The next attempt to upgrade the statue's lighting system began in May 1916, when it was under the control of the War Department. At the time, Ralph Pulitzer, Joseph's son, was operating the *World*. He led a fund drive to raise money (thirty thousand dollars) to pay for a lighting system designed and installed by General Electric. The system used 246 floodlights with 250-watt bulbs at the base of the statue. The torch was to be lit up by 15 lamps of 500 candlepower.

Gutzon Borglum, who would later go on to sculpt Mount Rushmore, made the modifications to the torch. Borglum cut out six hundred sections of the statue's copper flame and replaced them with amber-tinted glass. Although it looked like an over-size lamp to some observers, it did increase the torch's visual effect. However, the glass squares were not properly sealed, causing water to leak into the torch and arm whenever it rained. The result was irreparable corrosion that caused the torch to be replaced in the 1980s.

President Woodrow Wilson attended the inauguration ceremony for the new lighting system. On the evening of December 2, 1916, he flipped a wireless switch that turned on the new system. Even though the *World* had failed to raise enough money via nickels and dimes (the total was only met through the last-minute intervention of millionaire Henry Latham Doherty), the new lighting system was in place and working perfectly. The lights also eliminated shadows that were forming the appearance of bags under the Statue of Liberty's eyes and another that made the statue seem to have a double chin.

Details of the statue's arm and torch can be seen in this photo.

In 1931 another enhancement to the lighting system occurred. This time, eight one-thousand-watt lights were placed around the statue, and thirteen extremely bright floodlights were set around the rim of the torch. The lights were automatically turned on by a special radio signal.

Subsequent updates to the lighting system were made in 1944, 1976, and with the statue's complete overhaul in the 1980s. Each update has provided better lighting, and now it truly seems like the Statue of Liberty is capable of enlightening the world.

A MAJOR OVERHAUL

Even though the lighting system had undergone several modifications over the years, the statue itself had been ignored except

SPECIFICATIONS

The Statue of Liberty is one of the most impressive monuments in the world. Here are some of its measurements:

Total height: 306 feet
Statue height: 152 feet
Pedestal height: 154 feet
Length of arm holding torch: 45 feet
Head thickness: 10 feet
Eye width: 2 feet, 6 inches
Nose: 3 feet, 8 inches
Mouth width: 3 feet
Length of hand: 16 feet, 5 inches
Total weight: 560,000 pounds

when there was a problem that needed to be addressed. For example, in 1907 the first elevator was installed. In the late 1930s the steel supports for the crown's rays were replaced. Then, in 1946, the inside of the statue was given a new coat of paint.

However, in 1980, as a result of the unauthorized climb, officials decided to take a closer look at the overall condition of the statue because it was feared that the climbers had harmed it. In fact, a group of French experts were asked to help with the survey of the statue. In many ways this was appropriate since the statue was built by a Frenchman and was a gift from France. What they found was that the statue's skin and armature were in terrible condition, and immediate steps needed to be taken to avoid more serious problems, such as actual pieces of the statue falling off and plummeting to the ground. Professor Norman Weiss of the Columbia School of Architecture said it best when he noted, "Maybe this is the time to itemize problems with the statue. It's not like a building where you can do a little maintenance now and a little later. It will require a major investment of personnel and dollars."[40]

It was well known that the environment around the statue was spewing harmful, corrosive chemicals. Nearby coal-burning plants emitted oxides of sulfur and nitrogen that, when combined with moisture, caused acid rain that fell on the statue's copper skin. It had been feared that some of the plates had corroded to an almost paperlike thinness.

However, to everyone's great relief, the statue's copper skin was found to be approximately the same thickness. Furthermore, the statue had originally glowed like a shiny new penny. However, the combination of the environment and the chemicals in the air had turned the copper skin bluish green, called a patina. The patina provides copper with a long-term stability against atmospheric elements and reduces corrosion. Since some of the copper plates were visually or structurally unacceptable and had to be replaced, it was decided to accelerate the process that had turned the rest of the statue green. This would ensure that the new plates would not look out of place.

After examining the copper skin, the inspectors began an examination of the interior pylon. Although the inspectors found that it was structurally sound, they discovered that the internal "ribs" were corroding and needed to be replaced. A material called 316-L was chosen to replace the original iron. The inspectors also decided to replace the iron bars that connected the ribs to the pylon. To do so, a steel material called Ferralium 225 was selected. Because steel and copper can also produce a galvanic effect under certain extreme conditions, restorers used Teflon tape with a pressure-sensitive silicon backing as an insulator instead of asbestos.

Like the ribs, many of the rivets needed to be replaced. Many had popped out over the years, and moisture had seeped in through

Lady Liberty gets a facelift.

the vacant holes. In addition, one of the rays in the statue's crown had punched a large hole in her upraised arm because of an error in how the two were initially assembled. (It was not a problem with Bartholdi's original design.) Water was leaking into the statue from this hole as well. Some thought was given to correcting the century-old error by readjusting the ray, but ultimately it was decided to just repair the hole and reinforce the arm.

Unsightly cracks in the statue's nose were also repaired. These were fixed by the so-called wolf-mouth method of joining two large pieces of metal by way of cutting them into the shape of a sawtooth, making them level, interlocking them, and then hammering them together.

Perhaps most ironic, the much-maligned and much-repaired torch was deemed ruined beyond repair by all of the water that had leaked into it over the years. Because of the potential for chunks of it to fall and injure people below, it was decided to remove it and display it inside the statue. A new torch would be built following Bartholdi's original design—copper sheathing with no openings and gilded with gold to enhance its reflective characteristics. The gilding would take approximately five thousand gold sheets to complete.

A plan was also agreed on to modernize interior elements. To regulate humidity and heat and make it more pleasant for visitors, an air-conditioning system was needed. This would be most welcome on hot days, when the temperature inside the statue climbed to 110 degrees Fahrenheit. It would also reduce humidity, which was another source of condensation inside the statue. Another interior improvement would be the installation of a double-decker elevator. The stairs inside would also be widened and repaired.

A new gold-covered torch replaces the original one, damaged by time and the elements.

At the same time, some people began paying attention to the deplorable condition of Ellis Island, located just across the water. The island, which is an official part of the Statue of Liberty National Monument, was in terrible shape: Weeds were growing in courtyards, roofs were crumbling, and wreckage was strewn all over. It was decided that, as part of the statue's facelift, Ellis Island would also get refurbished.

THE COST OF LIBERTY

The French-American Committee for Restoration of the Statue of Liberty (as the formal organization was called) and the National Park Service realized they would need a lot of money to accomplish their task. When all of the figures were added up, it was determined that $230 million was needed to completely restore the Statue of Liberty, repair a few key buildings on Ellis Island, and perform some other tasks, such as rebuilding the Ellis Island wharf. Again, the federal government did not want to get involved. Like the original building of the statue, and the fund drive to raise money for the pedestal, money was going to have to come from private sources.

Given the lack of success of previous fund drives, there might have been some swiftly beating hearts when this new fund drive was launched on May 18, 1982. The group heading the funding effort was called the Statue of Liberty–Ellis Island Centennial Commission. It was headed by Lee Iacocca, the chairman of the Chrysler Corporation, who was much admired in America for the way in which he had pulled the troubled automaker back from the brink of bankruptcy. It was decided that the opening date of the money-raising effort would be July 4, 1984, and the closing date would be October 28, 1986.

Maybe it was the admiration for Iacocca, or the fact that America was a different nation from the one it was a hundred years ago, but the commission had no trouble raising the needed monies. Corporate sponsors like Coca-Cola and Eastman Kodak rushed to become involved, and by the end of the first year approximately $50 million had been donated by large corporations.

But not all of the money came from big companies. The commission made a deliberate effort to reach the people—after all, Lady Liberty was their statue—and it was rewarded with a flood of contributions. In fact, a "test letter" sent out to nearly five hundred thousand people in September 1983 was so successful, and generated so much money, that the committee decided not to wait for the official start of the fund drive but to go ahead and start raising money. In addition, the *New York Daily News* also began raising money for the statue, likening itself to the *World* of a century before. By the "official" start of the fund drive, July 4, 1984, over $100 million had been raised.

Accordingly, in January 1984 the first barge of construction materials was shipped to the statue, and the erection of the giant three-hundred-ton aluminum scaffolding that would eventually envelop the Statue of Liberty was begun. In late May 1984, the statue was closed to the public because of the construction, although Liberty Island (the name of Bedloe's Island had been changed in 1956) remained open. The statue would not reopen again for over two years.

Finally, on July 4, 1986, the statue was reopened to the public in time for its one hundredth birthday celebration later that year. The statue was as structurally sound as when it was first built.

Shrouded by scaffolding, the Statue of Liberty receives a thorough restoration in 1984.

THE APPEAL OF THE STATUE

The Statue of Liberty has called New York Harbor home for over a century. During that time it has watched millions of people come to the United States seeking a new life and new freedoms. For them, the sight of the statue standing proud and tall in the harbor has been the realization of their dreams of America.

The Statue of Liberty has stood unwavering as the United States changed. Once a country of manufacturing and farming, the United States has ushered in a whole new age of information and technology with the advent of electronics and computers.

The statue has also undergone its own transformation. Once merely a statue of copper representing a lofty ideal, it has become a symbol of the very nation it represents. Anyone who sees the Statue of Liberty understands its significance.

Sailboats throng New York Harbor on July 4, 1986, during the one hundredth anniversary celebration of the Statue of Liberty.

The statue draws people to it at all times. "Alone with God and the statue, Christmas Eve,"[41] was found scribbled on it during the 1984–1986 restoration. The National Park Service estimated that in the years before the statue was closed for refurbishing, twenty-five hundred people per day visited the statue.

Yet despite it all, the Statue of Liberty remains what it is—a statue dedicated to individual liberty. Notwithstanding all that has happened, it remains a monument to the concept that all people are created equal and are endowed with certain rights that no government can take away.

Notes

Chapter 1: A Dinner Party Conversation

1. Quoted in Christian Blanchet and Bertrand Dard, *Statue of Liberty: The First Hundred Years*. New York: American Heritage, 1985, p. 16.
2. Quoted in Jonathan Harris, *A Statue for America*. New York: Four Winds, 1985, pp. 4, 7.
3. Quoted in Blanchet and Dard, *Statue of Liberty*, p. 22.
4. Quoted in Blanchet and Dard, *Statue of Liberty*, p. 30.
5. Quoted in Harris, *A Statue for America*, p. 16.
6. Quoted in Blanchet and Dard, *Statue of Liberty*, p. 33.
7. Quoted in Blanchet and Dard, *Statue of Liberty*, p. 33.
8. Quoted in *Ellis Island and Statue of Liberty*. San Francisco: American Park Network, 1999, p. 62.
9. Quoted in Blanchet and Dard, *Statue of Liberty*, p. 36.
10. Quoted in Blanchet and Dard, *Statue of Liberty*, p. 36.
11. Quoted in Blanchet and Dard, *Statue of Liberty*, p. 36.
12. Quoted in Richard Seth Hayden and Thierry W. Despont, *Restoring the Statue of Liberty*. New York: McGraw-Hill, 1986, p. 21.
13. Quoted in Harris, *A Statue for America*, p. 14.
14. Quoted in Blanchet and Dard, *Statue of Liberty*, p. 40.
15. Quoted in Blanchet and Dard, *Statue of Liberty*, p. 41.
16. Quoted in Blanchet and Dard, *Statue of Liberty*, p. 48.

Chapter 2: A Slow Start

17. Quoted in Blanchet and Dard, *Statue of Liberty*, p. 51.
18. Quoted in Harris, *A Statue for America*, p. 45.
19. Quoted in Harris, *A Statue for America*, p. 46.
20. Quoted in Blanchet and Dard, *Statue of Liberty*, p. 52.
21. Quoted in Harris, *A Statue for America*, p. 67.

Chapter 3: Building a Dream

22. Quoted in Mary J. Shapiro, *Gateway to Liberty*. New York: Vintage Books, 1986, p. 19.
23. Quoted in Harris, *A Statue for America*, p. 29.

24. Quoted in Harris, *A Statue for America*, p. 39.

25. Quoted in Harris, *A Statue for America*, p. 79.

26. Quoted in Harris, *A Statue for America*, p. 55.

Chapter 4: Liberty Comes to America

27. Quoted in Blanchet and Dard, *Statue of Liberty*, p. 88.

28. Quoted in Blanchet and Dard, *Statue of Liberty*, p. 90.

29. Quoted in S. H. Burchard, *The Statue of Liberty: Birth and Rebirth*. San Diego: Harcourt, Brace, Jovanovich, 1985, p. 48.

30. Quoted in Harris, *A Statue for America*, p. 110.

31. Quoted in Blanchet and Dard, *Statue of Liberty*, p. 90.

32. Quoted in Harris, *A Statue for America*, p. 114.

33. Quoted in Harris, *A Statue for America*, p. 118.

34. Quoted in Blanchet and Dard, *Statue of Liberty*, p. 92.

35. Quoted in Harris, *A Statue for America*, p. 127.

Chapter 5: Lady Liberty: Decline and Restoration

36. Quoted in Blanchet and Dard, *Statue of Liberty*, p. 114.

37. Quoted in Burchard, *The Statue of Liberty*, p. 105.

38. Quoted in Burchard, *The Statue of Liberty*, p. 63.

39. Quoted in Harris, *A Statue for America*, p. 134.

40. Quoted in Burchard, *The Statue of Liberty*, p. 141.

41. Quoted in Hayden, *Restoring the Statue of Liberty*, p. 55.

For Further Reading

James B. Bell and Richard I. Abrams, *In Search of Liberty*. Garden City, NY: Doubleday & Crig, 1984. The story of the statue up to its 1980s restoration.

Lynn Curlee, *Liberty*. New York: Atheneum, 2000. The story of the statue from its inception at a dinner party in France to its dedication in America in 1886.

Paul C. Ditzel, *How They Built Our National Monuments*. Indianapolis: Bobbs-Merrill, 1976. The stories of all our national monuments.

Mary J. Shapiro, *Gateway to Liberty*. New York: Vintage Books, 1986. A book about the Statue of Liberty and Ellis Island.

Frank Spiering, *Bearer of a Million Dreams*. Ottowa, IL: Jameson Books, 1986. A history of the statue.

Gina Strazzabosco-Hayn, *The Statue of Liberty*. New York: Powerkids Press, 1998. Describes the planning and building of the statue.

Marvin Trachtenberg, *The Statue of Liberty*. New York: Viking, 1976. A history of how and why the statue was built.

WORKS CONSULTED

Christian Blanchet and Bertrand Dard, *Statue of Liberty: The First Hundred Years*. New York: American Heritage, 1985. A history of the statue from conception to its 1980s renovation.

S. H. Burchard, *The Statue of Liberty: Birth and Rebirth*. San Diego: Harcourt, Brace, Jovanovich, 1985. A book about the history of the statue.

Ellis Island and Statue of Liberty. San Francisco: American Park Network, 1999. A pamphlet about Ellis Island and the statue.

Oscar Handlin, *Statue of Liberty*. New York: Newsweek Book Division, 1971. A book about the statue and its role in America's freedoms.

Jonathan Harris, *A Statue for America*. New York: Four Winds, 1985. A complete recounting of the statue's history.

Richard Seth Hayden and Thierry W. Despont, *Restoring the Statue of Liberty*. New York: McGraw-Hill, 1986. The story of how the statue was restored in the 1980s.

Barry Moreno, *The Statue of Liberty Encyclopedia*. New York: Simon & Schuster, 2000. An exhaustive reference book about everything even remotely connected with the Statue of Liberty.

INDEX

95

Picture Credits

About the Author

Russell Roberts graduated from Rider University in Lawrenceville, New Jersey. A full-time freelance writer, he has published over two hundred articles and short stories and thirteen nonfiction books. Some of his book titles include *Stolen: A History of Base Stealing*, *Discover the Hidden New Jersey*, *101 Best Businesses to Start*, *Lincoln and the Abolition of Slavery*, and *Vampires*.

He currently resides in Bordentown, New Jersey, with his family and a fat cat named Rusti.